D0844427

RURAL EDUCATION AND TRAINING IN THE NEW ECONOMY

RURAL EDUCATION AND TRAINING IN THE NEW ECONOMY
The Myth of the Rural Skills Gap

Edited by

Robert M. Gibbs, Paul L. Swaim,
and Ruy Teixeira

IOWA STATE UNIVERSITY PRESS / AMES

© 1998 Iowa State University Press, Ames, Iowa 50014
All rights reserved

Iowa State University Press
2121 South State Avenue
Ames, Iowa 50014

Orders: 1-800-862-6657
Office: 1-515-292-0140
Fax: 1-515-292-3348
Web site: www.isupress.edu

LC
5146.5
.R87
1998

∞ Printed on acid-free paper in the United States of America

First edition, 1998

Library of Congress Cataloging-in-Publication Data

Rural education and training in the new economy : the myth of the rural skills gap—edited by Robert
    M. Gibbs, Paul L. Swaim, and Ruy Teixeira.—1st ed.
        p.   cm.
    Includes bibliographical references and index.
    ISBN 0-8138-2333-1 (alk. paper)
        1. Education, Rural—Economic aspects—United States.   2. Rural youth—Education—
United States.   3. Occupational training—United States.   4. Rural renewal—United States.
I. Gibbs, Robert M. (Robert Martin). II. Swaim, Paul L. III. Teixeira, Ruy.
    LC5146.5.R87   1998
    370′.9173′4—dc21   98-7060

The last digit is the print number: 9 8 7 6 5 4 3 2 1

CONTENTS

FOREWORD

This book makes an important contribution to countering questionable conventional wisdom, public perceptions and development strategies that have held sway in and about rural America for several decades. It uses new sources of information, incisive analysis and many new and different questions to describe rural students, schools, labor markets and economies in a brighter and more valid light. Neither a rural apology nor even rural advocacy, it just gathers up the pertinent facts and organizes and analyzes them in ways that provide a clearer educational and economic perspective on rural America—freed from the constraints of anecdote. It opens doors for rethinking conventional wisdom regarding the link between education and economic growth. It emphasizes that education and skill training without jobs, or sources of livelihood that use that education, is only half the story. It also emphasizes that the opportunity structure for rural youth and citizens is changing dramatically as we near the turn of the century. In 1998 population is growing as rapidly in rural as in urban America; contributing half that rural population growth is an 11 percent outmigration from metro areas between 1990 and 1995. A new economy fueled by new production and communications technologies has allowed cost of living and quality of life to become considerations in making new investments—considerations that favor many rural areas. With telecommunications technology it is possible for the producer's body to be located anywhere and the producer's mind to go forth and make a living. This book provides a basis for public policy and private decision makers to rethink the constraints of their conventional wisdom, inherited from an industrial past, about the role of human capital in both local and national economic development.

For many years the conventional wisdom passed on to rural youth by family, friends, counselors and teachers has been to stay in school, go on to college and from there to a city where the better paying jobs are located. Rural youth by the millions followed that advice and, in so doing, provided a steady stream of one of the most economically valuable exports from rural America—human capital. It is reasonable to assert that for many decades rural America has been subsidizing national economic growth through its export of natural resources and human capital even as rural communities and regions were having difficulty capturing a return on their human capital investments.

In some ways the migrating stream of the most highly educated from rural areas provided the title for an historically important report on poverty in rural

America, *The People Left Behind*. Correspondingly rural America was becoming known more for the people left behind than for its contribution of talent and treasure to urban based economic growth. The emerging strategy for rural development, from small community city halls to the halls of Congress, focused on attracting lower wage, lower skill manufacturers and other employers to rural areas. That strategy, especially during the 1960s and 70s, reinforced by public investments in infrastructure and local tax abatements, resulted in a massive industrial relocation elevating manufacturing to the top among sources of rural income and employment. Although the times and the economy have changed, this conventional wisdom and accompanying development strategies have been resistant to change.

Ironically although urban America had for decades welcomed with open arms the talents, skills and education of many rural migrants, the conventional wisdom of many policy makers, professional educators and analysts leaned in the direction of declaring rural schools to be inferior and therefore candidates for elimination and/or consolidation. Apparently the basis for those claims had more to do with rural/urban differences in inputs than outcomes. An important contribution of this book is its focus on outcomes regardless of the level of inputs. That analysis produces a different conclusion: rural schools and students generally fare as well as urban schools and students, and generally do so at less cost.

A part of the problem with past generalizations about rural America is that rural America defies generalization. In every respect rural America has become far more diverse than metropolitan America and its vast stretches of homogeneous suburbs. Rural America incorporates the nation's extremes of per capita income, culture, life style and occupation. In contrast to the sameness of the suburbs, rural communities and regions are more often economically specialized and take on some of the character of their dominant occupations, e.g. farming communities, logging communities, retirement communities, etc. As adaptation is being made to the new economy, a greater premium is being placed on strategies and institutions designed to serve the specific needs of specific places. The model of one size fits all, whether economic or educational, is being relegated to the past. In that context this book provides new perspectives, new analyses, and reinforcement to rural leaders and localities as they devise the ways they will fit into the new economy.

Daryl Hobbs
Professor of Rural Sociology
University of Missouri

INTRODUCTION

by Paul L. Swaim, Robert M. Gibbs, and Ruy Teixeira

THE CONTEXT

The one-room school house is a potent symbol of the high value Americans place on education. In earlier times, the small country school was an essential institution for providing a highly rural population with access to a basic education. The one-room school house survives as a cultural icon in a world more attuned to the pulses of digitized information than to the succession of the seasons. Unfortunately, today's small rural schools are more likely to be viewed as a weak link than as a progressive force when the prospects of rural people and places are assessed.[1]

Concern for the adequacy of rural schools is part of a larger unease that rural people and places may be disadvantaged in the evolving national economy. Of course, worries that rural schools lag the times and that rural communities face economic decline and depopulation are not new. These concerns acquired increased urgency, however, when the general vitality of rural areas during the rural renaissance of the 1970's was succeeded by economic setbacks and quickened outmigration of the 1980's. Some of these difficulties reflected transitory factors, such as the unsustainable debt burdens that resulted in the "farm crises" of the early and mid-1980's. And indeed, trends in the 1990's have been more hopeful, as real earnings stopped their long decline and the rural brain drain slowed. Despite these recent improvements, the rural landscape remains marked by large areas where the economic base has deteriorated and the promise of the information economy seems far removed.

Meanwhile, complex and rapidly changing technologies and intensified global competition are reshaping the American economy as a whole. Many wonder if rural workers and firms will be competitive in this "New Economy," one increasingly dominated by workers and firms with the information, skills, and other resources required to develop and apply advanced technologies and to pursue global competitive strategies. The apparent increase in the importance of advanced education and technical knowledge for competitive economic success also suggests that better education and job training have become essential elements of viable programs for rural economic revitalization.

Concerns for the competitiveness of local firms and the quality of the jobs that they provide are not limited to rural America. These concerns are also well-grounded in recent national economic experience. After rising rapidly during the 1950's and 1960's, average wages stagnated beginning in the early 1970's. Inequality among wage earners has also risen sharply, so that low-education, minority, and other vulnerable groups have experienced large wage declines. For example, male high school graduates in their first few years out of school earned 28 percent less in 1995 than in 1973, and high school dropouts fared even worse (Mishel, Bernstein, and Schmitt 1997). The relatively tight labor markets of the mid-1990's have meant jobs for most who want them, but they have not yet erased the wage erosion of the preceding two decades. Without a fundamental reversal of recent trends, there is a very real chance that many Americans entering the labor force in recent years will be poorer than their parents.

No single cause accounts for the declining availability of good jobs nationally, but inadequate workforce skills are widely believed to play an important role. During most of the 1980's, human capital concerns focused on the perceptions that American workers had too little schooling or that the quality of American public education was too low. More recent studies have also emphasized that most American firms do not provide their noncollege workforce with adequate job training and, in any case, do not organize production to make good use of the cognitive abilities of frontline workers (Commission on the Skills of the American Workforce 1990; Reich 1992). These later assessments depict the American economy as facing a choice between a high-skill, high-wage development path and a low-skill, low-wage path and advocate public policies encouraging firms to select "high-road" competitive strategies.

Recent federal policy has reflected these concerns. For example, President Clinton has often stated that expanding the supply of "good" jobs is a priority of his administration and has proposed fundamental reorganizations of high school–labor market linkages and public employment training programs in the belief that the American system of workforce preparation is inadequate for current needs. More recently, the president has supported tax credits for attending college in the belief that advanced education is a necessity, not a luxury, in the contemporary economy.

In addition to its human capital initiatives, the Clinton administration is directly assisting employers to adopt "high-road" competitive strategies, for example, through expanded funding for the Manufacturing Technology Centers administered by the National Institute of Standards and Technology of the Department of Commerce. Intense budgetary pressures, as well as ideological resistance to industrial policy, have greatly limited the scale and implementation of these federal initiatives. Although many states are also implementing or discussing similar reforms, it is difficult to get an overview of these efforts or to assess the likelihood that these decentralized measures will cohere into an effective national response. Despite the limited and fragmentary nature of these policy initiatives, much of American industry appears to have become more competitive since the early 1980's. The key question today is no longer if U.S. industry can develop viable strategies for remaining competitive, but rather how many American workers will have both the capacity and the opportunity to share in the gains from globalization and new production technologies.

Concern for low job quality has a special urgency for rural areas (Gorham 1992). During the 1980's, rural economic stress was highly visible in the form of plant closings, farm foreclosures, and high rates of unemployment. Less visible, but perhaps more symptomatic of a long-term worsening of rural employment opportunities, was the sharp decline in rural wages compared with urban. Between 1979 and 1990, average nonmetro earnings fell an inflation-adjusted 13 percent, while metropolitan wages fell less than 2 percent (Swaim 1995). As a result, the rural-urban gap in average weekly earnings rose from $71 to $122 (both figures in 1996 dollars), and the share of the rural workforce receiving poverty-level wages (wages so low that a full-time, year-round worker is unable to support a family of four above the poverty line) rose from 34 to 43 percent. Rural labor market conditions have improved since the 1990–91 recession, but it is not yet clear whether rural America is truly moving toward a high-skill, high-wage track or simply sharing in a strong business cycle expansion.

Rural education levels are lower than urban, and the economic trends outlined above were particularly unfavorable to low-education and rural workers. This coincidence suggests that the long-run deterioration of rural employment opportunities may be rooted in the inadequate skills of the rural workforce. However, a 1991 study by the Economic Research Service, which some of the present authors contributed to, casts some doubt on this reasoning and provides an important point of departure for our new study (McGranahan et al. 1991). The study showed that the high-skill, high-wage jobs created during the 1980's were disproportionately urban, a pattern that resulted in low demand for educated workers in rural areas and calls into question simple "supply-push" strategies for rural revitalization, which rely on increased years of schooling alone to generate large growth dividends. These findings did not contradict the idea that improved workforce skills are an important component of viable rural development strategies. But they did suggest that rural workforce quality is more complicated than fashionable pronouncements suggest, and that workforce quality and job quality are equally large obstacles to improved rural labor force well-being.

Is there an important skill gap that is holding back rural economic development? As the contributors to this collection probed deeper into the issue of skill supply and workforce preparedness, we began to realize that the rhetoric about rural skill gaps and low educational quality was often based on anecdote or fragmentary data. Until recently, national data on school quality and educational achievement simply were not obtainable. Within the past decade, several new surveys sponsored by the Department of Education have become available to the research community that are unprecedented in their content. These include major surveys of schools, teachers, students, and the literacy skills of adults. The Bureau of Labor Statistics filled another critical hole in the evidence by conducting new surveys of the job training received by the current workforce. A comprehensive examination of the rural skill development system has now become possible for the first time.

Much improved evidence of rural skill demand has also become available. Several recent national surveys provided valuable data about firms' use of new production technologies and forms of work organization, and their implications for skill demands and workforce training (Black and Lynch 1996; Frazis, Herz, and Horrigan 1995). Unfortunately, these surveys and related studies of industrial production technologies tend to ignore rural and urban differences or use methods of comparison not likely to detect the kinds of change now occurring in the rural workplace. In 1996, the Rural Manufacturing Survey, a national survey of establishments newly developed by the Economic Research Service, gave the most complete picture to date of rural employers' concerns about labor, changes in skill requirements, and the use of new production technologies and management practices. This survey, together with other data sources, provides the basis for a comprehensive examination of rural skill demand, which is a critical component of any assessment of the adequacy of rural skill supply in the current economic environment. The emergence of these unprecedented sources of data about rural skill supply and demand was the genesis of the present work.

HOW WE PROCEEDED

In undertaking this study, we have attempted to serve two purposes. The first purpose of our study is to contribute to the ongoing search for human capital initiatives that can make important contributions to rural economic development. Even though a simple supply-push development strategy is questionable, it is important to establish if—and how—more sophisticated skill-upgrading strategies can contribute to rural economic revitalization.

Employment will probably continue to fall in resource-intensive industries, such as farming and mining, and routine manufacturing, which have provided much of the rural economic base. A major challenge for rural development policy today is thus to create new or upgraded rural niches in the evolving national economy. And if such economic diversification and modernization strategies are to succeed, they frequently will need to include initiatives to upgrade workers' skills. Our analysis of rural skill supply and demand provides some of the information needed to identify more sophisticated skill-upgrading strategies, for example, by showing how the low literacy or lack of particular skills of certain groups of rural workers is a barrier for employers who are adopting skill-intensive, high-road competitive strategies, or might otherwise do so.

Our second motivation for studying the skill development system for rural workers reflects equity concerns. All rural youths deserve equal access to the life opportunities opened up by a good education and advanced vocational training, but some may face particular barriers to developing their human capital. The concern for equal access has become more urgent since the late 1970's because the labor market returns to education and job training have increased dramatically. Our comprehensive assessment of rural schools and job training provides a fuller understanding of the barriers preventing too many rural individuals from obtaining the skills needed to qualify for good jobs and suggests policies to lower those barriers.

Our approach assesses rural education and job training from the perspectives of rural people and of rural places. From the perspective of rural individuals, the basic question that we pose is "Do rural residents have adequate educational and vocational training opportunities?" In posing and analyzing this people-centered question, we implicitly assume that all rural residents should receive a good primary and secondary education and have the opportunity to pursue advanced education and job training, if they desire to do so and have the necessary ability. From the perspective of rural places, the basic question that we pose is "Does the rural skill development system supply the workforce competencies rural employers need to be competitive while paying high wages?" In posing and analyzing this place-centered question, we implicitly assume that rural economic revitalization is desirable and can be furthered by conscious efforts to adapt rural institutions and practices to changing conditions.

In the first and longer part of the book, which consists of chapters 1 to 6, we focus on skill supply. Our strategy for assessing rural education and job training is to follow rural individuals through important stages of their "careers" as learners. At each stage, we monitor educational progress and identify economic, social, and institutional factors that either assist their progress or prevent them from obtaining the skills and knowledge needed to participate fully in the evolving national economy. To the extent possible, we analyze the specific content of the skills that are learned by students or workers and compare these skills with evolving job requirements. The knowledge and insights that emerge help to answer both the people- and place-centered questions posed above, but the perspective is a little different in each case. When assessing the opportunity structures facing rural individuals, attention will typically focus on groups who lag in the quantity or quality of their learning and the inequities those patterns may reflect. When assessing rural education and training as they affect economic development, rural-urban discrepancies in skill supply assume center stage.

One benefit of our approach is that we develop much better measures of rural skills than were previously available. These measures allowed us to examine the assertion that rural workforce skills are inferior to urban. We find that this common perception is mistaken, in part, and masks important areas of strength in rural skill supply that can be built upon and more effectively tapped by rural development policy. Prior to our study, in fact, good measures of rural workers' skills simply did not exist. Average years of schooling typically had been relied upon to assess rural workforce quality, even though educational attainment is a poor indicator of the extent to which individuals possess the cognitive skills and technical knowledge required by more demanding (and better paying) jobs. Thus, we compile and analyze a number of additional measures of rural skills, such as educational achievement, adult literacy, and job training. The result is a much fuller portrait of the state of rural human capital, as well as new insights into how the rural skill development system could be strengthened.

Our study provides an analysis of rural workforce skills that is intended to provide a solid factual and theoretical foundation for assessing public and private initiatives to improve rural education and job training. Yet it would be incomplete without asking just how much difference a better-prepared rural workforce would make. If education and training are to be an effective component of a rural development strategy, that education and training must be matched with commensurate employer demand for skilled labor. The second part of the book, which consists of chapters 7 and 8, asks whether and to what extent this demand exists and, therefore, the extent to which worker skills are really a key barrier to increased competitiveness. A particularly important issue addressed in these chapters is whether the skill-intensive, high-road strategies—which were largely a monopoly of urban employers during the 1980's—are now being adopted by significant numbers of rural employers. Put more succinctly, are there any New Economy jobs for rural workers?

OVERVIEW OF OUR FINDINGS

The first three chapters focus on primary and secondary education. In the first chapter, Ballou and Podgursky analyze rural primary and secondary teachers and schools. They find that rural schools are relatively poor in terms of certain resources but appear to function more effectively than urban schools, perhaps due to their smaller sizes and fuller integration with the surrounding community. Greenberg and Teixeira examine educational achievement in the second chapter and find that—despite a lesser availability of advanced courses—rural high school seniors receive an education comparable in quality to that of urban students. The third chapter, by Paasch and Swaim, shows that rural dropout rates have improved dramatically in the last 20 years but a significant dropout problem persists, which is deeply rooted in the economic disadvantages of some students' families.

The second set of three chapters follow individuals beyond high school into their adult years. Gibbs examines college attendance and its relationship to migration in the fourth chapter. Higher education emerges as a significant weak link in the rural skill development system. In the fifth chapter, Greenberg, Swaim, and Teixeira analyze the literacy and "numeracy" of rural adults and find that there is only a modest gap between the literacy of the rural and urban adult workforces as a whole, a gap that is largely attributable to older workers who grew up at a time when rural education lagged urban. Swaim assesses job training in the sixth chapter and identifies and analyzes a rural gap in training for incumbent workers that emerged during the 1980's.

The final chapters investigate employers' demand for labor and their perceptions of the rural workforce. Teixeira and McGranahan in Chapter 7 report results from a national manufacturing establishment survey, newly developed by the Economic Research Service. Rural manufacturers report rising skill requirements and consider labor quality to be their most pressing problem. However, only a progressive subset of high adopters of new technology are especially concerned with the lack of specific skills (i.e., problem-solving and noncomputer technical skills) and the difficulties they encounter in recruiting highly educated staff. Indeed, the quality that rural employers as a whole find most lacking, reliability, would seem impervious to changes in school or training quality. McGranahan and Ghelfi's reprise of their 1991 study in Chapter 8 finds new strength in the rural economy. Rural areas continue to specialize in routine manufacturing and other types of employment that make relatively little use of highly educated workers, but the progressive centralization of high-skill jobs appears to have halted during the 1990's. Their analysis suggests that rural employers are beginning to follow, if in a limited way, the high-skill path deemed vital to future prosperity.

We designed the book to be a comprehensive survey of rural education, training, and skills, in the hopes that its "one-stop" nature would enhance its usefulness. Working from so many different data sources and focusing on a variety of subgroups within the population, we anticipated conclusions that often contradicted one another. We were prepared to describe a multifaceted message, and certainly, some of the most important lessons to be learned are found among the subtle nuances of the analyses. Still, the findings from these eight chapters show remarkable cohesion, with a number of easily identifiable common themes.

A first theme is that the rural skill development system is a complex composite of troubling weaknesses and surprising strengths. Rural gaps in higher education and job training are examples of the areas of weakness, which may be of increasing importance for economic development. Certain rural groups, including minorities and southerners, also lag significantly in terms of their human capital.

On the other side of the ledger, an impressive rural strength is that rural grade schools and high schools appear to do as good a job educating their students as urban schools, with fewer resources. Indeed, national education and literacy surveys, as well as ERS's new manufacturing survey, suggest that the basic cognitive skills of typical rural workers match up well with those of their urban counterparts and do not appear to pose a significant handicap—relative or otherwise—to most employers. Another area of rural strength is two-year colleges that specialize in vocational education. Rural educational and development policies can and should build on these strengths.

A second theme is that institutions matter. For example, the effectiveness of rural schools exceeds what might be predicted based on the resources available to them. Ballou and Podgursky offer tantalizing clues about the origins of these hidden advantages, but further research is clearly called for to clarify their nature. Similarly, our analysis indicates that the smaller size and remoteness of rural firms constitute a barrier to job training, which sometimes can be ameliorated by public programs, such as outreach programs from two-year colleges. It is also increasingly clear that the implementation of high-road competitive strategies by rural firms involves much more than simply hiring more educated workers and paying them higher wages. Rural development policy should foster an environment that is conducive to more firms making the complex and interrelated adjustments necessary in areas such as technology use, work organization, and marketing strategy.

A third theme is that rural skill supply and its relationship to rural economic development can best be understood by also considering rural skill demand. During the 1980's, low rural demand for skilled workers was an important bottleneck constraining rural economic development. The labor market reward for rural workers who acquired a university degree, or simply good literacy and numeracy skills, was far lower than for urban workers. In such an environment, supply-push development policies that seek to raise workforce skill levels are unlikely to be very successful because few workers or firms would perceive a significant economic return to additional investments in human capital.

Chapters 7 and 8 show that the 1990's are different and that rural areas are starting to participate in a more equal way in the emerging New Economy. Reflecting this, skill requirements in rural areas are rising fairly rapidly for a set of skills—computer, interpersonal/teamwork, and problem-solving—that are not traditionally covered by the education and training system. And, among "high adopters" of new technologies and management practices, the demand for such skills is rising exceptionally rapidly and leading to fairly high incidences of reported skill deficiencies (though no higher in rural than in urban areas). A related development is that the wage premium rural firms are willing to pay for college graduates has jumped. These changes suggest that rural participation in the New Economy is growing and can be further expanded but that future gains depend less on remedial skill training for large segments of the rural workforce than on encouraging the acquisition of advanced academic training and cutting-edge "new skills" by a subset of workers. The great challenge the rural education and training system now faces is to better meet these needs, at the top of the skill distribution, while also addressing equity concerns for the entire workforce.

Note

1 Throughout this book, the term "rural" is often used interchangeably with "non-metropolitan" or "nonmetro." Unless otherwise indicated, the data descriptions and analyses delineate rural areas according to the county-based definition of "nonmetropolitan" approved by the Office of Management and Budget of the United States Government.

References

Black, S.E. and L.M. Lynch. 1996. How to Compete: The Impact of Workplace Practices and Information Technology on Productivity. U.S. Department of Labor, Washington, DC.

Commission on the Skills of the American Workforce. 1990. America's Choice: High Skills or Low Wages. Rochester, NY: National Center on Education and the Economy.

Frazis, H.J., D.E. Herz, and M.W. Horrigan. 1995. Employer-Provided Training: Results from a New Survey. Monthly Labor Review 118(5):3–17.

Gorham, Lucy. 1992. "The Growing Problem of Low Earnings in Rural Areas." In Rural Poverty in America, edited by Cynthia Duncan. New York, NY: Auburn House.

McGranahan, David A., Linda M. Ghelfi, Molly S. Killian, Timothy S. Parker, Paul L. Swaim, and Ruy Teixeira. 1991. Education and Rural Economic Development: Strategies for the 1990's. Washington, DC: U.S. Department of Agriculture, ERS Staff Report No. AGES 9153.

Mishel, Lawrence, Jared Bernstein, and John Schmitt. 1997. The State of Working America, 1996–97. Washington, DC: Economic Policy Institute.

Reich, Robert B. 1992. The Work of Nations: Preparing Ourselves for 21st Century Capitalism. New York, NY: Vintage Books.

Swaim, Paul L. 1995. "Rural Earnings Holding Steady in the Early 1990's." In Rural Conditions and Trends, Vol. 6, No. 1. Washington, DC: U.S. Department of Agriculture, ERS, pp. 18-21.

Rural Education and Training in the New Economy

CHAPTER 1

RURAL TEACHERS AND SCHOOLS

by Dale Ballou and Michael Podgursky

INTRODUCTION

A survey article on education policy in Organization for Economic Cooperation and Development (OECD) countries has described education in rural communities as a neglected "ugly duckling" (Sher 1983). Education research, particularly research on school reform, has focused primarily on urban schools (DeYoung 1987). In part, this is a reflection of the population mix: most students are enrolled in urban or suburban schools. No doubt it also reflects public concern with the highly visible problems of American cities. Finally, the urban focus may also reflect the belief, common among school reformers of the early twentieth century, that the "best practice" in pedagogy and administration would emerge in consolidated and professionalized urban school systems, rather than in backward rural ones (Tyack 1974).

More recently, attention has begun to turn back to rural schools. To some extent this stems from concern with rural economic development and the role that education and training can play in preparing the workforce for an era of rapid technology change. In addition, some educational researchers have argued that small rural schools can in fact provide lessons for urban school reform (Barker and Gump 1964; Hobbs 1989, 1995). Indeed, the literature on school reform often emphasizes the benefits of small school size, particularly for disadvantaged students (Goodlad 1984; Friedkin and Necochea 1988).

Unfortunately, research on rural schools has been hampered by a relative lack of data; only recently have data for nationally representative samples of rural teachers and schools become available. These new data bases, developed by the National Center for Education Statistics, now make possible more extensive and systematic comparison of rural and urban schools (Stern 1994). This chapter taps one such source, the 1987–88 Schools and Staffing Survey, to investigate differences between rural and urban schools. Consistent with earlier studies, we find that rural schools are indeed smaller and less specialized than their urban counterparts. In addition, they appear to be at a disadvantage in recruiting the most highly qualified teachers. As a result, rural schools do not offer as rich a curriculum to their students.

This loss of curricular diversity is not, however, the whole story. In several respects, rural schools appear to offer a learning environment superior to that available in other communities, particularly large urban centers. Classes are smaller. Students have greater opportunity for contact with their teachers, who in turn enjoy greater control and autonomy in the classroom, express significantly greater satisfaction with work, and report fewer classroom problems than do their urban counterparts.

DATA

This chapter is based on data drawn from the 1987–88 Schools and Staffing Survey (SASS). SASS is a comprehensive survey of approximately 9,300 public and 3,500 private school administrators and about 56,000 public and 11,500 private school teachers at these same schools. SASS contains four survey instruments: a school survey, a district-level survey focusing on teacher demand and shortages, an administrator survey, and a teacher survey. Response rates were quite high for public schools and public school teachers: 92 and 86 percent, respectively (for details on the 1987–88 SASS survey and methodology, see U.S. Department of Education 1992).

We have merged various data on community characteristics into the SASS file. One such variable, which plays a very important role in this study, is a 10-category code indicating a county's position along a rural-urban continuum ("Beale code"). To provide more reliable statistics, we have collapsed these categories into three classifications for metropolitan areas (central city, suburb, small city) and two nonmetropolitan classifications (small town, remote rural). Table 1.1 describes the resulting geographical categories and reports the share of schools and students in each.[1]

SCHOOL SIZE AND PROGRAM OFFERINGS

In 1940 there were 117,108 public school districts in the United States. By 1960 this number had fallen to 40,520, and by 1990 it had essentially leveled off at 15,367 (U.S. Department of Education 1993). Pressures for this massive rural

TABLE 1.1. Locational classifications

Classification	Beale Code	County characteristics	Percent of schools	Percent of students	Students per school
Metropolitan					
Central city	0	Central counties of metropolitan areas of 1 million population or more	18.6	24.7	688.0
Suburb	1	Fringe counties of metropolitan areas of 1 million population or more	14.5	16.0	570.3
Small city	2	Counties in metropolitan areas of 250,000 to 1 million population	31.5	33.3	549.1
	3	Counties in metropolitan areas of less than 250,000 population			
Nonmetropolitan[a]					
Small town	4	Urban population of 20,000 or more, adjacent to metropolitan area	20.8	17.2	430.4
	5	Urban population of 20,000 or more, not adjacent to a metropolitan area			
	6	Urban population of less than 20,000, adjacent to a metropolitan area			
	8	Completely rural, adjacent to metropolitan area			
Remote rural	7	Urban population of less than 20,000, not adjacent to a metropolitan area	14.5	8.9	317.7
	9	Completely rural, not adjacent to a metropolitan area			

[a]Although the code 8 counties are completely rural (that is, contain fewer than 2,500 urban residents), their proximity to metro areas appeared to provide a more urban environment, and they are therefore grouped with the more urban nonmetro counties in the "small town" category. We grouped the somewhat urban, nonadjacent, nonmetro counties, code 7, with the rural, nonadjacent metro counties, code 9, because their lack of proximity to metro areas appeared to provide a more rural environment. This grouping is named "remote rural" for ease of reporting.
Source: Butler and Beale (1994) and authors' calculations from the 1987-88 Schools and Staffing Survey.

consolidation came from "above"—for the most part from education profession-als and administrators in state education departments who considered small dis-tricts and schools inadequate, inefficient, and decidedly unprofessional. Of course, for these education departments it is easier to monitor and regulate 100 consolidated districts than 1,000 localized ones.

While this sweeping consolidation largely eliminated the one-room school-house, Table 1.1 shows that considerable differences between the sizes of rural and urban districts persist. As apparent in the last column, the average remote rural school enrolls only half as many students as a central city school. This difference is most pronounced at the secondary level, where the average rural school size is roughly one-third that of the typical urban high school.

Rural school district consolidations were undertaken, at least in part, to provide better educational opportunities and a wider range of services for rural students. While there has doubtless been progress in this respect, SASS data on the allocation of teacher time indicate that students in rural schools are less likely to benefit from specialized programs and advanced courses. In Table 1.2 we present a breakdown of student time spent in various programs of study.[2] High school students in remote rural communities and small towns are less likely than their counterparts in metro areas to be enrolled in special programs for the gifted or remedial instruction. They are also less likely to be taking an advanced math class (advanced algebra, analytical geometry, trigonometry, or calculus) or a science course beyond biology (physics, chemistry) than are suburban students, though in this regard they appear to be no worse off than other students in metro areas. Only a very small fraction of students in remote rural areas receive instruction in computer programming or other uses of computers, though this is also true of students in other types of communities. Interestingly, more student time is spent in advanced placement (AP) courses in nonmetro areas, even though evidence available from other sources suggests than fewer rural schools offer such courses (see Chapter 3).[3]

On the whole, the evidence in Table 1.2 confirms the conventional wisdom that rural schools offer their students a less rich, less diverse curriculum, though it should be stressed that, as far as mathematics and science training are concerned, differences are pronounced only when rural students are compared with the most favorably situated students in metropolitan areas, i.e., suburban resi-

TABLE 1.2. Percent of student hours spent in special and advanced courses[a]

| Program | Metro | | | Nonmetro | |
	Central city	Suburb	Small city	Small town	Remote rural
	Percent				
Advanced math	2.4	3.4	2.7	2.4	2.7
Advanced science	7.2	9.0	8.3	7.8	6.9
Computer programming	0.6	0.8	0.9	1.0	0.7
Advanced placement	4.0	4.0	4.3	4.7	4.6
Gifted	3.6	3.4	2.6	2.5	1.1
Remedial	5.5	4.8	5.1	3.9	2.8

[a]High school students only. Calculations are based on the allocation of teacher time, weighted by the number of students with whom each teacher dealt in each period.
Source: Calculated by the authors using data from the 1987-88 Schools and Staffing Survey.

dents. How great the need for specialized programs is, of course, still another question.

In Table 1.3 we present evidence on the incidence of various programs by type of community. The dependent variables—collected at the school level—differ slightly from the measures in Table 1.2, insofar as they represent the percent of the student population enrolled in the program in question, rather than the fraction of student hours involved. Given that such measures are available at the school level, it is possible to perform a statistical analysis controlling for other school-level characteristics that proxy the demand (need) for such services.

Our controls include the level of the school (elementary, middle, secondary, combined), the percent of students eligible for free or reduced-price lunch, and the percent of students who are black or Hispanic. The results suggest that, after adjusting for these factors, nonmetro schools do offer fewer specialized services compared with schools in metro areas. Interestingly, the share of the student body in college preparatory courses is no smaller in remote rural schools than in central city or suburban schools, a result consistent with the data on advanced placement enrollment. Rural schools have smaller shares of students in bilingual and English as a second language (ESL) programs (controlling for the percent of Hispanic students), an indication that this population receives different services as a function of location. The earlier findings in Table 1.2 with respect to enrollment in remedial and gifted programs are confirmed here.

TABLE 1.3. School courses and services (relative to central city schools)

	Metro		Nonmetro	
Dependent variables	Suburb	Small city	Small town	Remote rural
Percent of students in:				
College preparatory courses	0.1	7.2***	-7.4***	1.7
Bilingual courses	-3.6***	-3.4***	-4.4***	-3.4***
English as a second language (ESL)	-0.6	-2.8***	-3.7***	-4.1***
Remedial reading	-3.7***	-2.2***	-2.2**	-2.3***
Remedial math	-2.8***	-2.2***	-2.7***	-2.9***
Gifted programs	0.4	-1.2***	-2.0***	-1.9***
Vocational or technical programs	-1.1	0.2	2.0	1.8
Percent Chapter 1 students	-3.6***	-10.2	-10.3	-10.8
Percent receiving diagnostic services	-0.9	-0.5	-1.7**	-1.0

Notes: The unit of observation is schools (n = 6,894). These estimates control for school level and the percent of students eligible for free lunch, percent black, and percent Hispanic. The values reported above represent the difference between the percent for each area and the central city percent for each item.

***,**,* denote statistically significant differences at 1, 5, and 10 percent confidence levels, respectively.

Source: Calculated by the authors using data from the 1987-88 Schools and Staffing Survey.

RURAL TEACHERS AND OTHER STAFF

While rural schools typically offer less diverse programs, they also provide offsetting advantages. Some of these benefits are depicted in Table 1.4, which presents the ratio of students to teachers and other staff in various communities. Particularly noteworthy are the differences in student/teacher ratios. We report two measures. One is the number of students at the school divided by the number of teachers (in full-time equivalents). Since this ratio can be heavily influenced by the presence of teachers with specialized assignments who deal with very small numbers of students, we present an alternative measure—the number of students taught on an average day by high school instructors of departmentalized subjects (e.g., English, history). By both measures, it is clear that rural students benefit from a more favorable student/teacher ratio. Indeed, the typical high school teacher in a remote rural school has only three-fourths as many students as an instructor in a central city or suburban community. Rural schools also have lower ratios of students to principals, guidance counselors, and other staff.

Lower teaching loads probably help rural schools in their effort to recruit good teachers. However, earlier research has often emphasized the difficulty of recruiting adequately trained teachers to rural areas, the quality of the rural teaching workforce, and looming "teacher shortages." (Darling-Hammond 1984; Dunathan 1980; Swift 1984). Low salaries are frequently cited as a contributing factor (Horn 1985). In Table 1.5 we report two measures of teacher pay in rural and urban schools: average pay offered beginning teachers (whose highest degree is a B.A.) and average salaries for teachers holding an M.A. with 20 years experience.[4] Not surprisingly, wealthier metro areas tend to pay teachers more than the less affluent towns and rural communities. Since costs of living also tend to be higher in urban areas, the comparison of nominal salary levels is less instruc-

TABLE 1.4. Ratios of students to teachers and other staff by residence

	Metro		Nonmetro		
	Central city	Suburb	Small city	Small town	Remote rural
Total number of students taught on an average day (HS)	104	99	96	85	75
			Ratio		
Students/teachers	21.2	17.8	18.6	17.3	16.0
Students/principal	272	267	242	202	126
Students/guidance counselors	516	578	465	491	405
Students/librarians	639	500	460	436	332
Students/other professional staff	323	263	358	526	442
Students/teacher aides	84	84	79	66	60

Source: Calculated by the authors using data from the Schools and Staffing Survey, 1987-88.

tive than it might be. Thus we have also adjusted teacher pay for differences in cost of living, deflating by a state-level metro-nonmetro cost of living index.[5] While nominal pay for starting teachers is 21 percent higher in central cities than in remote rural areas, the computed adjusted gap is considerably smaller at 8 percent. The gap widens considerably for experienced teachers, where nominal pay is 35 percent higher and adjusted pay 20 percent higher in central cities.

Interpretation of such rural-urban pay gaps is complicated given the mix of amenities (and "disamenities") in rural versus urban areas and the wide dispersion of individual preferences regarding these amenities. In a competitive labor market, mobility decisions are determined not just by pay, but by locational and job amenities as well. Thus, the fact that a science teacher in rural Montana earns $25,000 while a similar teacher in Chicago earns $40,000 does not necessarily mean that the former would prefer to swap jobs with the latter (or vice versa). In fact, as we will see below, rural teachers are no more or less satisfied with their pay than are urban teachers, and they are much more satisfied with their work environment. Thus much of the observed rural-urban pay gap may reflect a compensating differential for teaching and living in a urban setting.

TABLE 1.5. Teacher pay in urban and rural schools, 1987-88

	Starting out[a]		Experienced[b]	
	Nominal	Adjusted	Nominal	Adjusted
		dollars		
Metro				
Central city	20,030	17,836	35,398	31,566
	(121.2)	(107.9)	(134.9)	(120.3)
Suburb	19,084	16,960	34,251	30,577
	(115.5)	(102.6)	(130.5)	(116.5)
Small city	17,834	16,596	30,039	28,022
	(107.9)	(100.4)	(114.5)	(106.8)
Nonmetro				
Small town	17,024	16,943	27,560	27,464
	(103.0)	(102.5)	(105.0)	(104.6)
Remote rural	16,530	16,530	26,245	26,245
	(100.0)	(100.0)	(100.0)	(100.0)

[a]B.A. degree and no previous experience.
[b]M.A. degree and 20 years experience.
Notes: Adjusted figures control for cost of living differences between county types (McMahon and Chang 1991). An index for teacher salaries using the remote rural category as the base is reported in parentheses.
Source: Calculated by the authors using data from the 1987-88 Schools and Staffing Survey.

Whether these community amenities fully offset pay differentials may be gauged by comparing the characteristics of metro and nonmetro workforces. As shown in Table 1.6, rural teachers are somewhat younger than their urban counterparts. Remote rural schools have relatively more male teachers but considerably fewer black or Hispanic teachers. Rural teachers are also more likely to be married and tend to have more children than their urban counterparts.[6]

The rural-urban pay gaps may also reflect the much lower levels of unionization in rural districts. Teaching is one of the most highly unionized occupations. Table 1.7 reports unionization rates by school district. Teachers in urban districts, especially suburban ones, are far more likely to be covered by collective bargaining agreements than are teachers in small towns or remote rural districts. Only 49 percent of remote rural districts have collective bargaining agreements with their teachers. This compares with 81 percent of central city and 87 percent of suburban districts. It is also interesting to note that the informal "meet and confer" model, which affords less leverage to teacher unions, is more prevalent in the rural districts.

Since rural teachers are somewhat younger than urban teachers, it is not surprising that they also have somewhat less teaching experience. They tend to have more years of experience at their current school, however, at least compared with teachers in central city schools. This clearly suggests that interschool mobility of rural teachers is lower. Annual rates of teacher turnover (reported at the school) are quite high in both rural and urban areas, and only slightly lower in rural schools.

Does this teacher turnover present greater difficulties for rural schools? Is there a "teacher shortage" in rural schools? SASS asked districts to indicate the number of advertised teaching positions that were left unfilled or that were filled by a substitute as of October 1. The highest incidence of such vacancies occurred in central city schools, where .8 percent of all teaching positions were still waiting to be filled by qualified permanent personnel. The incidence was even lower in other areas and was smallest in remote rural areas and small towns (.47 percent and .45 percent, respectively).[7]

These figures do not support the claim that rural schools are unable to recruit qualified teachers. However, when teachers who lack appropriate certification credentials cannot be hired, state regulations usually allow for "temporary" or "provisional" certification. Thus, the incidence of unfilled positions may fail to reflect fully the problems faced by rural schools in recruiting instructors. The proportion of teachers with less than full certification in their primary teaching assignment should provide additional information regarding shortages. As shown in Table 1.6, virtually all teachers hold standard certification in their principal field. The ratio is as high in remote rural and small town districts as it is in the suburbs and small cities and exceeds the percent in central cities.

While the evidence strongly suggests there is no absolute shortage of teachers, districts in metro areas may nonetheless have a better applicant queue from which to select. We report several measures of the academic credentials of teach-

TABLE 1.6. Characteristics of full-time teachers

Characteristic	Metro			Nonmetro	
	Central city	Suburb	Small city	Small town	Remote rural
	Percent				
Male	30.0	31.3	28.1	29.5	32.2
Black	17.1	4.6	7.7	6.3	5.0
Hispanic	5.8	1.7	3.3	1.5	1.9
Married	66.5	73.7	77.1	77.3	77.8
Turnover rate[a]	10.4	9.5	9.7	9.1	9.7
Certified[b]	93.5	97.1	96.6	96.7	96.8
M.A.	45.0	46.8	40.1	36.9	32.3
Ed.D./Ph.D.	1.3	0.8	0.6	0.5	0.4
Graduate of a selective college[c]	24.5	26.9	19.1	15.3	12.1
B.A. in academic field[d]	42.1	39.3	34.3	31.3	28.3
B.A. in math or science	12.5	12.5	10.7	10.6	9.3
	Number				
Average number of children	1.0	1.1	1.1	1.2	1.2
	Years				
Age	42.7	42.2	41.3	40.5	40.4
Full-time experience	16.4	16.9	15.8	15.1	15.3
Full-time tenure at current school	8.9	9.7	8.9	9.4	9.7

[a]Turnover is the number of teachers who left during the 1986-87 academic year divided by the number of teachers employed as of October 1987.
[b]Certified is holding standard state certification in the primary subject taught.
[c]Selective colleges are those defined as "most," "highly," or "very" competitive in Barron's *Profiles of American Colleges* (1990).
[d]Teacher received a bachelor's degree in the academic field taught, rather than or combined with a degree in education.
Source: Calculated by the authors using data from the 1987-88 Schools and Staffing Survey.

TABLE 1.7. Collective bargaining in urban and rural districts

	Collective bargaining	Meet and confer	None
	Percent		
Metropolitan			
Central city	81.0	7.0	12.0
Suburb	86.5	4.0	9.5
Small city	73.0	4.8	22.2
Nonmetropolitan			
Small town	57.9	7.7	34.4
Remote rural	49.1	9.6	41.3

Source: Calculated by the authors using data from the 1993-94 Schools and Staffing Survey.

ers in Table 1.6. Rural teachers are less likely to have graduate degrees or to have graduated from a "selective" college or university than their urban counterparts.[8] While research on education production functions has failed to establish a strong relationship between the level of a teacher's highest degree and his or her effectiveness in the classroom, there is stronger evidence that persons who attended better undergraduate institutions are more capable teachers, ceteris paribus. (This literature is reviewed in Ballou and Podgursky 1997.) The fact that a remote rural teacher is only half as likely to have graduated from such a program suggests that rural districts are at a relative disadvantage in recruitment.

Concern about the low standards for admission to teacher education programs, as well as a new emphasis on academic rigor in undergraduate education, has led a number of states to require that prospective teachers at the secondary school level major in the subject they are to teach. In this light, we compare the academic preparation of teachers by community in Table 1.6. Nonmetro secondary school teachers are less likely to have majored in an academic subject (as opposed to education) than are secondary school instructors in metro areas. In particular, central city and suburban teachers were a third again as likely to have majored in math or science, areas where the shortage of adequately trained instructors has been considered to be particularly severe.

To summarize, the evidence made available by the SASS suggests that rural schools have not been able to staff their schools with teachers whose academic background and professional preparation equal those of central city and suburban instructors. This is particularly apparent when we look beyond formal teaching credentials to indicators of the quality of undergraduate education and subject matter knowledge. While lower salaries may hamper rural recruitment, adjusted pay for beginning teachers in remote rural communities is on average only 8 percent below that of new teachers in central cities. Thus, the rural disadvantage likely reflects other difficulties in recruiting teachers (many of whom are second wage earners in their families) to communities offering limited employment opportunities to spouses.

SCHOOL ENVIRONMENT

While the comparison of rural with urban schools has tended so far to confirm the impression that rural communities offer their youth inferior educational opportunities, the SASS teacher survey also provides extensive data on teacher assessments of the school environment. It is here that we find several striking differences between urban and rural schools, differences that suggest that rural schools offer a learning environment equal to or better than that available in urban areas.

In tables 1.8 through 1.10 we present results of an analysis of survey items pertaining to teachers' perceptions of school environment. Table 1.8 reports information on teachers' assessments of various problems at their schools. We report regression coefficients from a model in which the dependent variable was the teacher's response to various statements about the school. Possible responses ranged from 1 = serious problem to 4 = not a problem, so that a positive value represents a more favorable assessment, relative to central city schools. Independent variables, in addition to the type of community, included teacher demographic characteristics and experience, school level, and the socioeconomic status of the student population (as measured by the proportion of students eligible for free lunches, and the race and ethnic composition of the student body). The pattern of responses shows that on almost every count remote rural schools provide a more attractive learning environment than do central city school systems. On 10 of 13 problems, ranging from student tardiness and absenteeism to student possession of weapons and verbal and physical abuse of teachers, remote rural teachers gave their schools better marks than did central city instructors. In only two cases, student pregnancy and student use of alcohol, did remote rural teachers report a more serious problem than their counterparts in central cities. While differences between remote rural and other metropolitan districts are less pronounced, it is noteworthy that on virtually every item, remote rural schools also rated better than suburban and small city systems.

Table 1.9 reports regression coefficients from an analysis of teacher assessments of various aspects of school organization. (Since the allowed responses ranged from 1 = strongly agree to 4 = strongly disagree, on favorable items a negative coefficient indicates a more favorable assessment.) Nonmetro teachers feel they have more contact with the principal regarding instructional practice. Compared with central city teachers, nonmetro teachers feel the principal provides more effective support with respect to discipline (row 7). In general, rural principals are seen as weaker "leaders" in the sense that they do not define the type of school they want and communicate it. The reason for this is not hard to find. Rural teachers seem to have much more autonomy in the classroom and more influence over school policy. As suggested by row 16 of Table 1.9 and the last five rows of Table 1.10, rural teachers enjoy significantly more control over their classrooms with regard to choice of textbooks, course content, teaching techniques, homework, and discipline. They also indicate that they have greater influence on school policy (row 10 in Table 1.9 and rows 1-2 of Table 1.10).

Other aspects of the teaching environment stand out as well. Rural teachers report more cooperative and collegial relationships with their fellow teachers, and less frustration with paperwork and routine duties. Remote rural teachers report that they receive more support from parents, and are more likely to find necessary resources such as textbooks and supplies available as needed. As noted above, although the nominal pay of rural teachers is much less than that of their central city counterparts, they report equal satisfaction with their salaries.

The assessments of teachers suggest that rural schools display many of the critical features identified in the "effective schools" literature. (Purkey and Smith 1983). What accounts for this rural advantage? One factor is school size. A significant theme in the recent school reform literature is that larger schools and

TABLE 1.8. Teacher assessments of school problems (relative to teachers in central city schools)

Problem	Metro		Nonmetro	
	Suburb	Small city	Small town	Remote rural
Student tardiness	.287***	.236***	.335***	.425***
Teacher absenteeism	.216***	.144**	.171***	.272***
Student absenteeism	.156***	.139***	.186***	.227***
Students cutting class	.215***	.164***	.210***	.242***
Physical conflicts among students	.270***	.179***	.211***	.294***
Robbery or theft	.216***	.132***	.147***	.227**
Vandalism of school property	.232***	.177***	.229***	.324***
Student pregnancy	.084***	-.031**	.141***	-.113***
Student use of alcohol	-.034***	.060***	.166***	-.179***
Student drug abuse	.037**	-.002	-.026*	.025
Student possession of weapons	.185***	.109***	.165***	.216***
Physical abuse of teachers	.160***	.136***	.189***	.219***
Verbal abuse of teachers	.271***	.203***	.267***	.370***

Notes: Teachers were asked to "indicate the degree to which each of the following matters is a problem in this school" and were given four possible responses to select, 1 = serious problem, 2 = moderate, 3 = minor, and 4 = not a problem.

These estimates control for school level, years of teaching experience, teacher demographic characteristics (sex, race, hispanic ethnicity, age), percent of students at school eligible for free lunch, percent black, and percent Hispanic. The values reported above represent the difference between each area's score and the central city score for each item

***,**,* denote statistically significant differences at 1, 5, and 10 percent confidence levels, respectively.

Source: Calculated by the authors using data on full-time teachers from 1987-88 Schools and Staffing Survey.

school districts display diseconomies of scale, which stifle innovation and adaption in school and classrooms (Walberg and Walberg 1994). Rural schools being on average smaller than urban schools may account for the differences in teacher assessments observed in tables 1.8–1.10.

In order to assess the effect of school size on our findings, we reran the 40 regressions underlying tables 1.8–1.10, adding a control for school size. This tended to reduce the rural advantage, but on virtually every question a significant rural advantage persisted. Something other than school size accounts for the rural school difference.

We also explored the question of regional differences in rural effects by reestimating the models with region dummy variables and an interaction term for rural southern teachers. This specification thus divided rural teachers into southern rural teachers and nonsouthern rural teachers. Southern rural teachers tended to be less satisfied with their salaries, resources availability, and class size

TABLE 1.9. Teachers' assessments of school organization (relative to teachers in central city schools)

	Metro		Nonmetro	
Item	Suburb	Small city	Small town	Remote rural
Principal talks with me frequently about my instructional practices	-.030	-.111***	-.130***	-.202***
Principal lets staff know what's expected of them	-.002	.049***	.022	-.002
School administrator behavior is supportive and encouraging	-.087***	-.104***	.072***	-.087***
Teachers are evaluated fairly	-.074***	-.055**	-.043***	-.049***
Principal knows what kind of school he/she wants	-.045**	.062***	.035**	.001
Goal and priorities of school are clear	-.051***	-.005	.003	-.008
Principal enforces school rules for conduct and backs me up	-.149***	-.098***	-.142***	-.120***
Student misbehavior interferes with my teaching	.211***	.181***	.195***	.243***
Rules for student behavior are consistently enforced	-.082***	-.102***	-.111	-.140***
Teachers participate in making most important educational decisions	-.078***	-.101***	-.074***	-.130***
I receive a great deal of support from parents	-.148***	-.086***	-.094***	-.228***
Routine duties and paperwork interfere with my teaching	.111***	-.048***	.020	.123***
Most of my colleagues share my beliefs/values about school mission	-.029***	-.079***	-.078***	-.101***
Cooperative effort among staff	-.080***	-.103***	-.089***	-.130***
I make an effort to coordinate content of my courses with other teachers	-.059***	-.024*	-.030**	-.078***
I have to follow rules that conflict with my best professional judgement	.069***	.083***	.067***	.110***
Necessary materials are available as needed by the staff	-.128***	-.083***	.067***	.110***
I am satisfied with my teaching salary	.051***	-.005	.003	.008
I sometimes feel it is a waste of time to try to do my best as a teacher	.114***	-.031*	-.007	.020
If you could go back to your college days would you become a teacher again?	-.069***	-.072***	-.078***	-.067**

Notes: Teachers were given four possible responses to select, 1 = strongly agree, 2 = somewhat agree, 3 = somewhat disagree, 4 = strongly disagree, except for the last question, where possible responses ranged from 1 = certainly would to 6 = certainly would not.

These estimates control for school level, years of teaching experience, teacher demographic characteristics (sex, race, hispanic ethnicity, age), percent of students at school eligible for free lunch, percent black, and percent Hispanic. The values reported above represent the difference between each area's score and the central city score for each item.

***,**,* denote statistically significant differences at 1, 5, and 10 percent confidence levels, respectively.

Source: Calculated by the authors using data on full-time teachers from 1987-88 Schools and Staffing Survey.

TABLE 1.10. Teachers' assessments of their own influence in the school and classroom (relative to teachers in central city schools)

	Metro		Nonmetro	
Item	Suburb	Small city	Small town	Remote rural

At this school, how much actual influence do you think teachers have over school policy in:

Determining discipline policy	.161***	.089***	.124***	.143***
Establishing curriculum	.319***	.203***	.370***	.396***

At this school, how much control do you feel you have in your classroom over:

Selecting textbooks and other instructional materials	.290***	.183***	.556***	.700***
Selecting content, topics, and skills to be taught	.206***	.158***	.454***	.581***
Selecting teaching techniques	.087***	.092***	.137***	.200***
Disciplining students	.162***	.067***	.107***	.184***
Determining the amount of homework to be assigned	.046**	.115***	.163***	.217***

Notes: Teachers were given six possible responses to select, from 1 = none, to 6 = a great deal. These estimates control for school level, years of teaching experience, teacher demographic characteristics (sex, race, hispanic ethnicity, age), percent of students at school eligible for free lunch, percent black, and percent Hispanic. The values reported above represent the difference between each area's score and the central city score for each item.

***,**,* denote statistically significant differences at 1, 5, and 10 percent confidence levels, respectively.

Source: Calculated by the authors using data on full-time teachers from 1987-88 Schools and Staffing Survey.

than their nonsouthern rural counterparts. Not surprisingly they were less satisfied with their teaching careers and less likely to report that they would, if given a chance, choose teaching as a career. On the other hand, they generally reported more input on various aspects of school policy. Southern rural teachers tended to find more problems in the learning environment of the type listed in Table 1.8. Thus the rural school advantages are rather more muted in the South. Of course, controlling for southern school district strengthens the contrasts between nonsouthern rural teachers and all other metropolitan or nonmetropolitan teachers. From the teachers' point of view, rural schools outside of the South provide a very attractive learning and teaching environment.

CONCLUSION

What factors can account for these rural school advantages? To a considerable extent, the positive assessments given rural schools reflect features of rural and small town life rather than schools per se. Schools mirror the communities in which they are situated. If crime and violence are problems in the community, surely they will spill over to the school as well. As one rural educational researcher writes: "Rural communities are still basically homogeneous, stable, and traditional, and rural schools remain essentially an expression of community life" (Dunne 1977, p. 91). Even though we have controlled for poverty rates and percentages of minority students in our statistical analysis, these variables do not perfectly proxy the range of problems besetting a community. Rurality will therefore continue to be associated with positive features of family and community life that support the efforts of local educators.

While omitted community characteristics can explain some of the results in tables 1.8–1.10, they cannot readily explain all of the significant differences in teacher control, cooperation, and collegiality we have identified. It is likely that the organization and management of schools play a part (Rosenfeld and Sher 1977; Tyack 1974; Nachtigal 1982). Urban and rural school models address the agency problem (i.e., how parents and taxpayers induce their agents, the teachers and principals, to serve them effectively) in fundamentally different ways. The approach taken in urban schools is hierarchical and bureaucratic, with decisions regarding textbooks, curricula, teaching methods, and discipline centralized and imposed on all the staff. Rural schools tend to leave these decisions in the hands of teachers, but the performance of the teachers is more effectively monitored and motivated by the closer ties between the school and the community. Teachers in rural school districts, for instance, are more likely to live in the community served by their school.[9] Thus bad teachers cannot as readily escape censure at the end of the day, while good teachers may find their superior performance continually reinforced. This also means that the children of rural school teachers are also more likely to attend the school at which they teach. Such close links between the teachers, the principal, the school board, and the community may lessen some problems of performance monitoring and motivation that beset all organizations.[10]

This contrast between rural and urban environments is starkly apparent in the way teachers allocated their time. Table 1.11 presents a breakdown of the hours teachers devote to their jobs the week prior to the administration of the SASS. (Our comparison focuses on instructors in secondary schools, where there is a wider range of activities involving students and teachers and where demands on teacher time for class preparation and student evaluation are likely to be greater.) Rural teachers spend approximately the same time in class preparation and student evaluation as urban instructors—indeed, more, when these figures are adjusted for differences in the student/teacher ratio. However, there is a striking contrast in the allocation of hours outside school to activities involving students. Remote rural instructors average a full 90 minutes more per week in such activities as coaching, drama, debate, and club sponsorship than do central city teachers.

Thus the relationship between the school and the community is a two-way

TABLE 1.11. Allocation of teacher time in secondary schools

	Metro			Nonmetro	
	Central city	Suburb	Small city	Small town	Remote rural
Home preparation, including grading	7.6	7.6	7.6	7.4	7.2
In-school preparation periods	6.1	6.5	6.2	6.1	5.9
After school activities involving student contact	4.0	4.2	4.6	5.0	5.5

Source: Calculated by the authors using data on full-time secondary school teachers from the 1987-88 Schools and Staffing Survey.

street, with the school both contributing to and benefiting from the greater sense of community and shared purpose found in rural and small town districts. The following characterization of the nation's Catholic high schools might well be applied to rural school systems:

> [T]he academic structure of Catholic high schools is embedded within a larger communal organization ... [A] set of distinctive structural components ... enable the community. Chief among these is an extended scope of the role of the teacher. Teachers are not just subject-matter specialists whose job definition is delimited by the classroom walls. Rather, they are mature persons whom students encounter in the hallways, playing fields, in the school neighborhood, and sometimes even in their homes. In the numerous personal interactions that occur among adults and students outside of classrooms, many opportunities are afforded for expressions of individual concern and interest. (Bryk and Lee 1993).

Just as the high quality of social interactions between adults and students has been found to contribute to the effectiveness of parochial schools, so it is reasonable to conclude that students in rural school systems also benefit from the more extensive contacts with their teachers that rural communities foster.

NOTES

1 The definition of rural counties in Table 1.1 is narrower than the subjective definitions employed by survey respondents. Only 33 percent of schools that administrators described as rural in the SASS survey actually fit our definition, which emphasizes remoteness from metropolitan areas. Indeed, 22 percent of schools that administrators classified as rural were, in fact, in counties with a metropolitan area of 250,000 or more.

2 SASS does not survey students or administrators on the courses taken by the former. The entries in Table 1.2 were obtained by summing the hours teachers spent instructing each of the various types of classes, weighted by the number of students in the class. By summing overall teachers in a sector (central city, suburban, etc.), we obtain an unbiased estimate of the fraction of student class time spent in each instructional program.

3 The most likely explanation for the apparent discrepancy is that more rural students take AP courses when their schools offer them. Unfortunately, the available data do not allow a direct test of this conjecture.

4 Since virtually all school districts follow "single salary schedules" (i.e., pay teachers at all levels and specialties according to a single schedule based on seniority and educational credentials), we do not disaggregate pay by school level.

5 The Bureau of Labor Statistics does not at present publish an index that would permit calculation of a real wage gap. The estimates in Table 1.5 use cost-of-living indexes prepared by the Center for the Study of Educational Finance at Illinois State University (McMahon and Chang 1991).

6 Given the sparsity of population in these rural counties, this means that rural teachers are more likely to have or have had their own children attend the teachers' schools. Of course, the same means that rural teachers are also more likely to live in the community in which they teach. We will return to the issue of community links.

7 This was not because remote rural and small town districts canceled positions they could not fill: cancellations were only .33 percent of all full-time equivalent (FTE) positions in rural districts, the same percentage as in suburban systems.

8 Selective institutions are those rated "most competitive," "highly competitive," or "very competitive" by Barron's Profiles of American Colleges, 1990. These categories include the main campus of the state university in most states, so it should not be assumed that rural districts simply lack the opportunity to hire such teachers. Nonetheless, it is true that the rural disadvantage is due in part to the fact that disproportionately many rural districts are located outside areas (e.g., New England) with a high concentration of selective colleges.

9 A survey by the National Education Association (1987, p. 173) found that teachers in smaller school districts were much more likely to live in the attendance area of the school in which they teach. Among teachers in districts with less than 3,000 students, 54.6 percent lived in the attendance area of the school. This compares with just 16.9 percent of teachers in districts with 25,000 or more students.

10 It should also be noted that collective bargaining is much less prevalent in nonmetropolitan districts (Table 1.7). Recent research by Hoxby (1996) has highlighted the negative effect of teacher collective bargaining on educational productivity.

REFERENCES

Ballou, Dale and Michael Podgursky. 1997. *Teacher Pay and Teacher Quality.* Kalamazoo, MI: W.E. Upjohn Institute for Employment Research.

Barker, Roger G. and Paul Gump. 1964. *Big School, Small School: High School Size and Student Behavior.* Palo Alto, CA: Stanford University Press.

Barron's Profiles of American Colleges. 1990. Hauppauge, NY: Barron's Educational Series, Inc.

Bryk, Anthony and Valerie Lee. 1993. "Lessons from Catholic High Schools on Renewing Our Educational Institutions." *Network News and Views* 12, no. 6:18–39.

Butler, Margaret A. and Calvin L. Beale. 1994. *Rural-Urban Continuum Codes for Metro and Nonmetro Counties, 1993*, USDA-ERS-RED, Washington, DC, September.

Cole, Robert. 1989. "Small Schools: An International Overview," EDO-RC-89-12. Charleston, WV: ERIC/CRESS Appalachia Educational Laboratory (September).

Chubb, John E. and Terry M. Moe. 1990. *Politics, Markets, and America's Schools*. Washington, DC: The Brookings Institution.

Darling-Hammond, Linda. 1984. *Beyond the Commission Reports*, R- 3177-RC. Santa Monica, CA: Rand Corporation.

DeYoung, Alan J. 1987. "The Status of Rural Education Research: An Integrated Review and Commentary." *Review of Educational Research* 57, no. 2 (Summer):123–48.

Dunathan, Arni T. 1980. "Teacher Shortage: Big Problems for Small Schools" *Phi Delta Kappan* (November):205–6.

Dunne, Faith. 1977. "Choosing Smallness: An Examination of the Small School Experience in Rural America." In *Education in Rural America: A Reassessment of Conventional Wisdom*, edited by J.P. Sher. Boulder, CO: Westview.

Friedkin, Noah and Juan Necochea. 1988. "School System Size and Performance: A Contingency Perspective." *Education Evaluation and Policy Analysis* 10, no. 3:237-49.

Goodlad, John I. 1984. *A Place Called School: Prospects for the Future.* New York: McGraw Hill.

Hobbs, Daryl. 1989. "Rural School Improvement: Bigger or Better?" *Journal of State Government*, pp. 22–28.

———. 1995. "Capacity Building: Re-examining the Role of the Rural School." In *Investing in People: The Human Capital Needs of Rural America*, edited by Lionel Beaulieu and David Mulkey. Boulder, CO: Westview Press.

Horn, Jerry G. 1985. *Recruitment and Preparation of Quality Teachers for Rural Schools*. Washington, DC: U.S. Department of Education.

Hoxby, Caroline M. 1996. "How Teacher Unions Affect Education Production." *Quarterly Journal of Economics* 115:671–718.

McMahon, Walter W. and Shao-Chung Chang. 1991. "Geographical Cost of Living Differences: Interstate, Intrastate, Update 1991." Center for the Study of Education Finance. Illinois State University, Normal, IL (April).

Nachtigal, P.M. 1982. *Rural Education: In Search of a Better Way.* Boulder, CO: Westview.

National Education Association. 1987. *Status of the American Public School Teacher: 1985–86.*

Purkey, Stewart C. and Marshall S. Smith. 1983. "Effective Schools: A Review." *The Elementary School Journal* 83, no. 4 (March):427–52.

Rosenfeld, Stuart A. and Jonathan P. Sher. 1977. "The Urbanization of Rural Schools, 1840-1970." In *Education in Rural America: A Reassessment of Conventional Wisdom*, edited by J.P. Sher. Boulder, CO: Westview.

Sher, Jonathan P. 1983. "Education's Ugly Duckling: Rural Schools in Urban Nations." *Phi Delta Kappan* 64, no.4 (December):257- 62.

Stern, Joyce D. (editor). 1994. *The Condition of Education in Rural Schools.* Washington, DC: Government Printing Office (June).

Swift, Doug. 1984. "Finding and Keeping Teachers: Strategies for Small Schools." Los Cruces, NM: ERIC Clearinghouse on Rural Education and Small Schools (September).

Tyack, David. 1974. *The One Best System: A History of American Urban Education.* Cambridge, MA: Harvard University Press.

U.S. Department of Education. Office of Educational Research and Improvement. 1992. *Schools and Staffing in the United States: A Statistical Profile 1987–88*, NCES 92-120. Washington, DC: Government Printing Office (July).

_____. National Center for Education Statistics. 1993. *Digest of Education Statistics, 1993*. Washington, DC: Government Printing Office (October).

Walberg, Herbert J. and Herbert J. Walberg III. 1994. "Losing Local Control." *Educational Researcher* 23, no. 5 (June–July):19–26.

CHAPTER 2

EDUCATIONAL ACHIEVEMENT IN RURAL SCHOOLS

by Elizabeth J. Greenberg and Ruy Teixeira

INTRODUCTION

The 1980's witnessed a troubling divergence of economic outcomes between urban and rural areas. This divergence included slower employment growth, higher unemployment, relative and absolute earnings deterioration, higher levels of underemployment, relative decline in rural per capita income, and higher poverty rates—trends that accentuated the basic rural-urban gap in living standards. And even in the 1990's, when economic trends have been more favorable in rural areas, this gap shows few signs of a quick reversal.

One possible explanation is that rural students receive an inferior education. Because of this, rural workers are not adequately prepared for the requirements of modern jobs, leading companies to locate elsewhere. This, in turn, lowers the employment opportunities and wages in rural areas. But the evidence for this point of view is thin and has generally been based on observations about relatively poor educational attainment (years of schooling) in rural areas. These observations are now seriously out-of-date, as evidence has accumulated that the educational attainment of the typical rural worker, particularly the young worker, has improved dramatically and is now very similar in rural and urban areas.[1]

However, it could be argued that educational achievement (what students actually learn in school) remains low in rural areas so that, despite increased years of schooling for rural workers and the marked convergence of high school completion rates, rural workers still receive an inferior education. In other words, the quantity of schooling rural workers receive has shot up, but the quality of that education remains exceptionally poor.

In this chapter, we will examine the hypothesis that rural education is markedly inferior by looking at the educational achievement of rural 17-year-olds, the cohort that is preparing to enter the labor market. Using data available from the National Assessment of Educational Progress we will compare test scores of rural 17-year-olds with those of urban 17-year-olds both at the present time and over the past two decades (the time period for which the data are available). Where data are available, we will also compare school-level characteristics, such as availability of advanced courses, across urban and rural areas.

In addition to comparing urban versus rural, which are quite broad categories, we will break the data down into finer categories based on proximity to cities and size of population (these categories, called "Beale codes," are described in the appendix to this chapter).[2] Finally, where possible, we will examine how achievement scores are affected by individual-level characteristics, such as number and education of parents at home, and school-level characteristics, such as advanced course availability and economic and demographic composition of the student body, to see whether differences between urban and rural schools are accentuated or blurred by such characteristics.

DATA

Most of the data in this paper come from the National Assessment of Educational Progress (NAEP), a survey of the cognitive achievement levels of 9-, 13-, and 17-year-old students across the United States. The survey started in 1970 and was conducted irregularly for the first few years, sometimes annually and sometimes biennially. Since 1978, however, the NAEP survey has been done regularly every other year.

The NAEP is the only existing data set that allows regular, statistically valid comparisons of achievement levels of students in the United States. Up to 100,000 students are tested during each survey year, distributed so that 4,000–6,500 students are tested in a given subject at each of the three age levels. Because our main interest is in the quality of the rural workforce, we focused our analysis on the 17-year-olds in the data set—the next cohort to enter the workforce.

The data we present in this paper go back to 1975 for reading, 1977 for science, and 1978 for math. We were unable to use the earliest NAEP surveys because we could not obtain county identifiers for the students that would allow us to make the geographical comparisons in which we are interested.

For the later years of the survey, 1986–94, we used the long term trend samples rather than the main samples of students. This is because, beginning in 1986, when the Educational Testing Service (ETS) took over the administration of the NAEP, the procedures used to administer the test, the time of year the test was given, and the way students' ages were measured were all changed. In order to allow comparison of the data with earlier years, ETS included a long term trend sample in each survey in which the test was conducted as it had been originally.

AVERAGE EDUCATIONAL ACHIEVEMENT, 1975–94

Comparing urban and rural NAEP scores for 1994, the most recent year for which we have data, we can see there is very little difference between the two groups (Table 2.1). Rural scores are somewhat higher in science, while urban scores are slightly higher in math and reading, but none of the differences are statistically significant at the 95 percent level of confidence.

Looking at the historical scores, the differences in achievement level between urban and rural have also been modest, though generally slightly larger in earlier years than in the current era. Thus, if anything, there has been some minor convergence of scores between urban and rural areas, rather than a divergence.

A simple comparison of urban and rural scores, therefore, indicates that there is little to worry about with regard to rural student achievement—at least in a relative sense. In fact, there appear to be grounds for optimism with regard to the accomplishments of rural students and schools.

TABLE 2.1. Average achievement scores of 17-year-olds by residence, 1975-94

Subject/area	1975	1980	1988	1990	1992	1994
Reading						
Urban	286.0	286.3	292.4*	290.9	290.6	288.5
Rural	283.5	282.8	285.4*	288.0	287.1	287.4
	1978	1982	1986	1990	1992	1994
Mathematics						
Urban	301.6*	299.8*	303.1*	304.6	307.4	306.7
Rural	297.4*	294.7*	299.1*	304.1	304.1	305.0
	1977	1982	1986	1990	1992	1994
Science						
Urban	290.0	283.4	288.3	289.6	293.7	291.9
Rural	287.5	284.7	288.8	291.7	293.7	298.3

*Urban-rural difference is significant at the 95 percent level of confidence. See the appendix to this chapter for definitions of scores.

Source: Calculated by the authors using data from the National Assessment of Educational Progress.

However, the categories urban and rural are so broad that they could cover up significant problems with some schools and students. For example, rural schools in the South have been an historical trouble spot in the educational system. Therefore, we also compared urban scores with rural when the data were divided into census regions.

Using census regions we see that there are in fact substantial variations among region/urban status categories, with southern students, in particular, scoring consistently lower than any other category of students (Table 2.2). However, within the South, the data show that the scores of southern rural students improved significantly over time in all three subjects, narrowing the gap in reading and almost closing it in science. But this is convergence at a relatively low level, since both southern rural and urban students in 1992 were still scoring below the national mean in all three subjects. There is no other geographic group for which this is true, and it should be a cause of concern to policy makers.

Looking at the other census regions, there was considerable over time improvement in all three subjects in rural areas in these regions (with the one exception of a 4 point decline in reading achievement in the rural Midwest). Combined with smaller and less consistent improvement in urban areas in these regions, the favorable trend in rural areas has led to an astonishing result: rural scores are now higher than urban scores in almost every instance in these regions (again there is only one exception, mathematics in the Northeast). This indicates that, outside the South, there is no longer an overall rural disadvantage in schooling. Indeed, in one subject, science, there is a consistently large (10–18 points) rural advantage.

We also broke the data down by Beale categories to see if the size or location of urban and rural areas has a significant impact on students' achievement. These results (Table 2.3) reveal some intriguing differences in students' achievement scores.[3]

As expected, the highest-performing urban category is the suburban category, while the lowest performing urban category is the central city category. But, while the highest-performing rural category—and the highest-performing category overall—is the one closest to urban areas (urban adjacent), the lowest-performing rural category is not one of the most rural categories, but rather one of the most urban (urban nonadjacent). Indeed, the latter category is the most poorly performing of all the Beale categories and shares, with the central city category, the dubious distinction of being substantially below the national mean in each subject in the last two assessments.

Thus, generally speaking, differences among Beale categories show no clear pattern related to rurality. Instead, there are strong and weak Beale categories in both urban and rural areas, and the strongest category of all actually turns out to be a rural one. This casts further doubt on the conventional assumption of a rural disadvantage in educational achievement.

The data in these tables show that trends in levels of educational achievement have brought rural and urban areas closer together over time. Indeed, outside the

TABLE 2.2. Average achievement scores of 17-year-olds by region and residence

Subject/area	1975	1980	1988	1990	1992	1994
Reading						
Northeast						
Urban	291.4	285.9	296.1	293.9*	298.8	296.5
Rural	287.9	281.8	292.4	304.1*	---	299.7
Midwest						
Urban	290.2	287.1	292.3	294.2	293.7	284.0
Rural	293.1	289.1	292.2	291.3	293.9	289.4
South						
Urban	278.6*	282.9	292.6*	289.1*	280.5	285.8
Rural	270.6*	276.1	278.0*	278.1*	279.6	280.9
West						
Urban	284.4	290.7	286.4	286.8	294.5	288.2
Rural	282.3	281.4	---	297.8	292.8	291.3

	1978	1982	1986	1990	1992	1994
Mathematics						
Northeast						
Urban	305.6	304.3	304.9	301.1	312.3	313.9
Rural	308.5	---	308.8	306.9	---	312.7
Midwest						
Urban	306.4	303.6	304.4	311.0	313.2	305.7
Rural	302.6	298.3	301.2	312.1	309.4	307.0
South						
Urban	295.7	293.6	302.7*	304.0*	301.4	303.8
Rural	290.5	287.5	296.5*	296.6*	299.7	298.5
West						
Urban	295.5	295.4	299.3	300.8*	305.2	303.6
Rural	296.9	297.5	295.4	312.6*	305.9	310.5

	1977	1982	1986	1990	1992	1994
Science						
Northeast						
Urban	295.4	283.1	287.7	288.4*	301.3	298.2
Rural	297.2	---	300.1	303.7*	---	307.5
Midwest						
Urban	293.4	290.0	293.8	298.3	304.7	292.8
Rural	296.8	288.6	296.2	303.5	303.5	305.0
South						
Urban	282.9*	278.1	288.3	286.3*	279.9	289.4
Rural	272.5*	275.4	284.7	278.9*	285.1	287.1
West						
Urban	287.3	280.8	280.9	284.8	296.0	287.4*
Rural	293.8	290.2	276.6	298.6	298.3	305.1*

*Urban-rural difference is significant at the 95 percent level of confidence for a given year in a given region. See the appendix to this chapter for definitions of scores.

--- = Insufficient number of cases to accurately compute statistic.

Source: Calculated by the authors using data from the National Assessment of Educational Progress.

TABLE 2.3. Average achievement scores by rural-urban continuum, 1975-94

Subject/area	1975	1980	1988	1990	1992	1994
Reading						
United States	285.6	285.5	290.1	290.2	289.7	288.2
Urban:						
Central city	279.1	283.0	291.1	284.5	282.5	282.2
Suburb	294.1	292.0	293.0	295.9	299.8	293.7
Medium	287.3	286.5	295.3	293.1	292.0	291.1
Small	286.9	282.7	291.7	290.7	289.5	285.0
Rural:						
Urban, adjacent	289.5	286.5	293.3	289.0	290.5	297.1
Urban, nonadjacent	287.8	287.2	285.2	298.3	279.1	276.2
Rural, adjacent	278.4	278.0	282.2	285.6	280.7	285.5
Rural, nonadjacent	284.0	281.7	283.4	285.8	291.4	287.3

	1978	1982	1986	1990	1992	1994
Mathematics						
United States	300.4	298.5	302.0	304.6	306.7	306.2
Urban:						
Central city	300.4	295.4	300.4	299.1	301.8	300.6
Suburb	301.7	310.1	306.8	309.3	314.5	313.2
Medium	305.4	299.1	304.9	306.6	306.2	309.0
Small	298.5	291.6	297.2	307.3	310.0	305.6
Rural:						
Urban, adjacent	300.6	295.6	306.5	309.2	305.2	311.2
Urban, nonadjacent	297.8	299.6	300.8	305.8	296.2	293.5
Rural, adjacent	294.0	294.8	297.1	299.8	303.3	304.1
Rural, nonadjacent	297.1	292.5	295.8	305.0	306.7	305.3

	1977	1982	1986	1990	1992	1994
Science						
United States	289.5	283.3	288.5	290.4	294.1	293.7
Urban:						
Central city	288.1	273.9	283.7	277.5	283.5	279.9
Suburb	297.3	297.2	295.9	298.2	303.7	298.1
Medium	288.5	283.7	287.9	294.9	292.7	298.5
Small	289.6	281.2	284.0	295.7	303.2	293.8
Rural:						
Urban, adjacent	296.9	283.7	293.5	298.1	297.2	305.1
Urban, nonadjacent	272.5	290.2	286.6	296.8	279.3	269.8
Rural, adjacent	284.6	282.7	288.1	284.9	290.7	297.8
Rural, nonadjacent	285.8	284.5	288.9	292.8	297.9	300.8

Source: Calculated by the authors using data from the National Assessment of Educational Progress.

South, these trends have actually produced a slight, but consistent, pattern of rural advantage, rather than disadvantage. This suggests that, while inferior education of rural high school graduates may once have been a possible—albeit minor—explanation for the failure of businesses to locate in rural areas, it can no longer be viewed as an adequate explanation for the continuing problems of rural development.

EDUCATIONAL ACHIEVEMENT BY RACE AND PERCENTILE

It could still be argued, however, that the aggregate results summarized in the previous section mask important trends among subgroups that would deter rural development, at least among certain populations. An obvious possibility here is that achievement trends among rural minorities lag those among rural whites, thereby threatening development prospects precisely where they are needed most.[4]

The data presented in Table 2.4 show clearly that, rather than being a source of concern, rural achievement trends among minorities are properly viewed as a source of strength. Among rural blacks, for example, average reading scores rose from 236 in 1975 to 260 in 1994, an increase of 24 points. In contrast, average reading scores among rural whites stagnated over the same period, rising only 1 point, from 290 to 291. Thus, instead of widening, the white-black reading achievement gap in rural areas has been substantially narrowed over time.

Achievement trends by race for math and science tell basically the same story. Thus, the trend data by race show that rural minorities, far from being left behind by achievement trends, are actually making more progress than their white counterparts.

A variant on the argument tested above is that aggregate rural achievement trends are masking differential trends at the bottom and top of the achievement distribution. For example, it is technically possible that the modest aggregate rural gain in achievement levels could include a substantial fall in achievement by the bottom 20 percent, which is then counterbalanced by a strong gain in achievement among the top 20 percent.

This hypothesis is tested with the data in Table 2.5. They show clearly that gains made by those at the bottom of the distribution have either been as large as those at the top (reading and science) or actually larger (math). In math, for example, achievement at the 20th percentile rises from 268 in 1978 to 281 in 1994, a gain of 13 points. In contrast, achievement at the 80th percentile rises only from 327 to 330 over the time period, a gain of 3 points. Thus, according to the table, the bottom is either rising faster than the top or rising at the same rate. This means that the differences among rural students are, if anything, declining rather than rising.

TABLE 2.4. Average achievement scores by race, ethnicity, and residence, 1975-94

Subject/area	1975	1980	1988	1990	1992	1994
Reading						
White						
Urban	293.6*	294.6*	297.2*	299.3*	299.7	297.6*
Rural	290.2*	287.3*	290.8*	291.7*	291.1	290.9*
Black						
Urban	240.0	244.4	278.9*	267.9	261.3	268.9
Rural	236.2	234.4	256.3*	258.7	257.6	259.7
Hispanic						
Urban	249.9	260.4	272.8	273.4	268.0*	262.2
Rural	---	265.8	260.2	280.9	282.1*	270.7
Other						
Urban	261.2	280.8*	285.5	289.9	287.1	284.7
Rural	259.2	259.9*	308.8	279.9	---	300.3

	1978	1982	1986	1990	1992	1994
Mathematics						
White						
Urban	307.6*	306.0*	309.4*	311.2*	313.0*	314.1*
Rural	301.4*	298.0*	302.3*	306.0*	308.5*	308.8*
Black						
Urban	269.3*	273.2*	279.6	287.3	286.3	287.3
Rural	262.0*	264.2*	279.8	290.5	275.4	280.0
Hispanic						
Urban	276.5	275.9*	281.8*	282.0*	291.2	290.9
Rural	273.0	282.4*	293.2*	293.4*	296.6	291.0
Other						
Urban	316.8	310.3	319.4*	314.4	320.6*	313.6*
Rural	302.6	295.3	285.5*	311.8	303.4*	274.7*

	1977	1982	1986	1990	1992	1994
Science						
White						
Urban	298.6*	294.3	297.9	302.3	305.6	306.1
Rural	294.5*	291.2	295.9	297.6	299.5	304.6
Black						
Urban	242.0*	236.4	253.3	253.3	255.7	258.5
Rural	234.2*	237.1	249.7	251.8	252.3	253.4
Hispanic						
Urban	262.3	248.0	258.5	260.7	261.3*	259.1
Rural	259.7	251.5	273.5	271.6	286.9*	278.1
Other						
Urban	291.6*	269.0	298.2*	293.3	286.0	287.5
Rural	273.5*	265.8	244.7*	281.5	299.2	271.0

*Urban-rural difference is significant at the 95 percent level of confidence for a given year.
--- = Insufficient number of cases to accurately compute statistic.
Source: Calculated by the authors using data from the National Assessment of Educational Progress.

TABLE 2.5. Rural achievement scores by percentile ranking of students, 1975-94

Subject	1975	1980	1988	1990	1992	1994
Reading						
20th	247.9	251.6	253.5	254.7	251.7	248.5
40th	275.3	274.7	276.9	279.7	279.0	275.5
60th	296.6	294.3	295.9	300.7	299.1	298.1
80th	320.4	316.5	316.8	322.8	320.2	321.2
	1978	1982	1986	1990	1992	1994
Mathematics						
20th	268.0	268.7	276.3	278.4	280.2	280.8
40th	288.3	286.4	291.3	296.6	296.8	296.6
60th	306.6	302.3	305.4	312.0	312.3	312.7
80th	326.8	322.1	321.8	328.8	329.2	330.1
	1977	1982	1986	1990	1992	1994
Science						
20th	251.4	247.0	254.3	256.3	258.0	261.2
40th	277.5	275.2	280.1	281.9	286.3	290.1
60th	299.4	297.2	299.7	304.1	305.8	312.9
80th	325.1	323.2	324.5	327.2	328.7	334.6

Source: Calculated by the authors using data from the National Assessment of Educational Progress.

COMPARING SCHOOL CHARACTERISTICS

Although the achievement levels of rural students are converging with those of urban students, rural schools still look different from urban schools. Specifically, rural high schools are significantly smaller than urban high schools, and on average they offer fewer advanced college preparatory classes.

For example, during 1994, 32 percent of rural students attended high schools with 400 or fewer students. Only 10 percent of urban students attended high schools this small. That same year, 31 percent of urban students attended schools with 1,500 or more students, while only 5 percent of rural students were in schools of this size.

The importance of school size is a subject of considerable debate in the education literature at the present. However, it is clear from our data that smaller schools do not have the resources to offer as many advanced courses as larger schools. For example, in 1994, only 59 percent of students in schools with 400 or fewer students were offered the opportunity to take calculus. But, when school size jumped to 1,000 or more students, 95 percent of students were offered the opportunity to take calculus. Similar patterns (though measured in earlier years) obtain for the availability of advanced science and other advanced placement courses by school size.

Given the relatively small size, then, of rural schools, it should come as no surprise that rural schools offer substantially fewer advanced classes than urban schools (Table 2.6). This is true for all subjects for which data are available, from English to calculus to chemistry, and except for one case (biology) the urban-rural gap is quite large, from 18 to 43 percentage points. Note however that NAEP data suggest school size may be only a partial explanation for the gap in course offerings between urban and rural schools. That is, controlling for school size—comparing urban and rural course availability for schools of similar size—fails to consistently eliminate this gap.[5]

Whatever the reasons for the gap, the fact remains that it is there and should be considered a serious problem. Indeed, it could be one important reason why rural students, despite their comparable academic achievement levels, are substantially less likely to attend college. This, in turn, hurts the future earnings prospects of these students and, perhaps, the development prospects of rural areas as a whole.[6]

EXPLAINING DIFFERENCES IN EDUCATIONAL ACHIEVEMENT

The previous sections describe the differences in educational achievement between rural and urban areas in considerable detail. We found that these differences are smaller than generally supposed, have been diminishing over time, and, in a number of instances, have actually turned into a rural advantage in educational achievement. This suggests that "rurality" is no longer a negative influence on the quality of education, if it ever was.

But it is possible that the descriptive statistics we are looking at mask the negative influence of rurality. That is, we may find that, once the influences of other

TABLE 2.6. Share of twelfth-grade students enrolled in schools that offer advanced curricula, 1994

Advanced courses	Urban	Rural
	Percent of all 12th-graders	
Biology	87.7	84.4
Calculus	93.2	64.2
Chemistry	74.8	56.9
English	81.9	41.2
History	69.5	26.4
Physics	63.6	33.7

Source: Calculated by the authors using data from the National Assessment of Educational Progress.

characteristics are controlled for—as can be done in a multivariate model—rurality does have a significant negative impact on educational achievement.

This possibility is tested by the data in Table 2.7. The first column under each subject shows the coefficients in a multivariate model[7] that includes only dummy variables for the eight Beale codes outside of completely rural areas. Essentially, this shows the extent to which average scores in these Beale regions—not controlling for other factors—are higher or lower than those in the most rural regions.

The second column under each subject shows coefficients for these same Beale regions, but from a multivariate model that includes a variety of predictors of educational achievement.[8] These predictors include the educational background of the student's parents, the race of the student, the gender of the student, the percent Hispanic in the student's school, the percent black in the student's school, the percent on welfare in the student's school, the region in which the student's school is located, the size of the student's school, and whether the student's school offers advanced courses in a subject (e.g., for mathematics, whether calculus was offered).

TABLE 2.7. Effects of area location on achievement, 1990

	Reading		Mathematics		Science	
Beale code	Location only	With predictors	Location only	With predictors	Location only	With predictors
			Coefficents[a]			
0	-3.68	-5.39	5.65	-2.95	3.41	-5.22
1	2.47	-6.07	14.65	-3.43	12.80	-7.90
2	-0.33	-2.36	9.97	0.02	9.16	-1.83
3	3.24	-2.09	4.64	-4.11	3.49	-2.66
4	2.53	-1.71	11.96	0.32	21.25	6.55
5	4.57	-3.51	13.62	2.11	10.96	-3.65
6	-4.30	-8.38	3.50	-4.75	-0.61	-13.15
7	-2.38	-3.87	0.35	-2.61	0.42	-2.88

Note: Effects are derived from OLS models without and with a series of control variables and are expressed relative to achievement in completely rural areas (Beale codes 8 and 9). Beale codes go from highest population density (0) to lowest population density (9) and are defined in the appendix to this chapter. Beale codes 0–3 are urban and 4–9 are rural.

[a] Standard errors for coefficients were estimated using a special procedure that corrects for ways in which the NAEP data deviate from standard OLS assumptions. As a result of this procedure, regular OLS standard errors are inflated to the point where it is quite difficult for coefficients to attain statistical significance. Reflecting this tendency, none of the coefficients displayed in this table were statistically significant at the 95 percent level of confidence, though many were in a model using regular OLS standard errors.

Source: Calculated by the authors using data from the National Assessment of Educational Progress.

The influence of the predictors themselves (not shown) was generally as expected.[9] Students whose parents had a college education did substantially better than those whose parents did not complete high school; white students did better than black students; students outside the South did better than those within the South; students in schools that offered advanced courses did better than those where such courses were not offered; and so on.

The interesting story does not lie with these predictors themselves, however, but rather—as implied by the structure of the table—with the changes in the Beale region coefficients once these predictors are added to the model. As can be seen in each subject, the Beale region coefficients tend to go from positive to less positive or negative, as one moves from column one to column two.[10] What this means is that, while achievement in completely rural areas may be lower than in other areas when other factors are not controlled for, once these factors are controlled for the rural disadvantage disappears and in many cases even becomes a rural advantage.

For example, in mathematics, the uncontrolled model (column one) shows all Beale regions having an achievement advantage over completely rural areas, ranging from .35 points (Beale category 7) to 14.65 points (Beale category 1). But the controlled model (column two) shows the worst rural disadvantage being only 2.1 points (Beale category 5) and shows an actual rural advantage over the majority of Beale categories (categories 0, 1, 3, 6, and 7).[11]

A similar pattern obtains in science achievement. And, in reading achievement, where even the uncontrolled model shows a rural advantage over several Beale categories, the controlled model shows a rural advantage over every single Beale category outside of completely rural areas.

What this means is very simple. Far from masking the negative impact of rurality, descriptive statistics actually overstate this negative impact and may even conceal a basically positive impact of rurality on educational achievement.

The underlying reason for this is that differences in the distribution of student and school characteristics (for example, parent's educational background, regional location, etc.) are more than adequate to explain observed differences between rural and urban achievement, without recourse to the allegedly negative influence of rurality. Indeed, if students in rural areas did not tend to have parents with poorer educational backgrounds, be disproportionately located in the South, lack access to advanced courses and so on, the data here suggest that rural students might generally outperform their urban counterparts (as indeed already appears to be the case in many areas of the country).

CONCLUSION

These findings suggests that an education-based explanation for rural development problems should be viewed skeptically. Not only have years of schooling increased dramatically for rural workers, the quality of that schooling actually improved relative to urban areas so that educational achievement in rural and urban areas is now roughly equal. This raises the possibility that the most serious skill obstacles to rural development may be on the demand side. This seems especially plausible in light of recent research indicating that the availability of high-skill jobs in rural areas, at least as conventionally defined, has been poor and will, at best, increase only slightly in the future.[12]

Is more and better education completely useless then? No, for two reasons. First, more and better education, even of a conventional variety, could still help individuals in rural areas. Second, if more education can be keyed to increasing demand for skills—perhaps the "new skills" (computer, problem-solving, teamwork) favored by high-tech firms[13]—rural areas could benefit from encouraging and meeting those skill demands.

This suggests that rural educational upgrading only makes sense as part of an integrated effort to boost rural demand for high-skill workers. Policies might include, for example, making rural areas more "urbanlike" by providing the information infrastructure needed to support the relatively high-skill sectors of the economy. But whatever the specifics, demand-oriented policies are clearly central to helping rural areas prosper in the twenty-first century.

APPENDIX

UNDERSTANDING NAEP SCORES

NAEP scores for the 17-year-olds in this study range from approximately 100 to 400. The meaning of the scores is as follows.

Reading

150: Can carry out simple, discrete reading tasks.
200: Can comprehend specific or sequentially related information.
250: Can search for specific information, interrelate ideas, and make generalizations.
300: Can find, understand, summarize, and explain relatively complicated information.
350: Can synthesize and learn from specialized reading materials.

Mathematics

150: Knows some addition and subtraction facts.
200: Can add and subtract two-digit numbers and recognizes relationships among coins.
250: Can add, subtract, multiply, and divide using whole numbers and can solve one-step problems.
300: Can compute with decimals, fractions, and percents; recognize geometric figures; solve simple equations; and use moderately complex reasoning.
350: Can solve multistep problems and use beginning algebra.

Science

150: Knows everyday science facts.
200: Understands some simple principles and has some knowledge, for example, about plants and animals.
250: Understands and applies general information from the life and physical sciences.
300: Has some detailed scientific knowledge and can evaluate the appropriateness of scientific procedures.
350: Can infer relationships and draw conclusions using detailed scientific knowledge.

RURAL-URBAN CONTINUUM (BEALE) CODES

We used rural-urban continuum codes (Butler and Beale 1994) to study differences among student scores by the level of urbanization of their home counties. We combined the four least urban rural groups into two categories because the NEAP sample was too small to produce reliable results for each of the groups separately. The groups analyzed are:

Name	Code	Description
Urban		
Central city	0	Central counties of metropolitan areas of 1 million population or more
Suburb	1	Fringe counties of metropolitan areas of 1 million population or more
Medium	2	Counties in metropolitan areas of 250,000 to 1 million population
Small	3	Counties in metropolitan areas of less than 250,000 population
Rural		
Urban, adjacent	4	Urban population of 20,000 or more and adjacent to a urban area
Urban, nonadjacent	5	Urban population of 20,000 or more and not adjacent to a urban area
Rural, adjacent	6 and 8	Urban population of less than 20,000 or no urban population and adjacent to a urban area
Rural, nonadjacent	7 and 9	Urban population of less than 20,000 or no urban population and not adjacent to a urban area

Urban and rural status is that announced by the Office of Management and Budget in June 1983, when population and commuting data from the 1980 Census of Population became available (except in the one case where we analyzed the 1994 NAEP data alone—for schools offering advanced courses—where we used the later 1993 codes instead). We chose to collapse the last four continuum codes by adjacency rather than level of urban population because the heavy reliance of the adjacent counties' workers on commuting to work in urban counties appears to distinctly differentiate them from the nonadjacent counties (Ghelfi and Parker 1997). Although these counties may have up to 19,999 urban residents, many of them have little or no urban population so we call them "rural, adjacent" and "rural, nonadjacent," for simplicity.

NOTES

1 See Teixeira (1995) for data and discussion.

2 In almost all of the analysis that uses Beale codes in this chapter, we use the 1983 codes to maintain comparability across time. However, in the final table (2.6), since it covers only the final year, 1994, we use the most recent codes available, issued in 1993.

3 In interpreting these scores it is important to remember that the sample size in some of the categories is small and many of the standard errors are large. What could be showing up in parts of the table, therefore, is fluctuation caused by sampling error. However, we have tried to confine our comments to results that are not tied to a sudden shift in any one category in any one year.

4 For more information on the situation of rural minorities, see the recent (1996) Economic Research Service monograph on the subject (Linda Swanson, ed.).

5 For example, in 1994, only 44 percent of students in rural schools with 400 or fewer children had the opportunity to take calculus, compared with 72 percent of urban students in schools of the same size.

6 See Teixeira (1995) and later chapters in this volume for more discussion.

7 Essentially, these are ordinary least squares (OLS) with the standard errors corrected to reflect the ways in which the NAEP data deviate from standard OLS assumptions.

8 These models were all estimated on 1990 data.

9 We did find that larger school size was generally a positive influence on student achievement, a finding that contradicts a number of recent studies on school size and achievement (see Stern 1994 and Chapter 1, Ballou and Podgursky, in this volume).

10 This same pattern obtains if one simply uses a single dummy variable (urban/rural) to capture the influence of rurality: the addition of predictor variables essentially eliminates negative effects of rurality on student achievement.

11 The same basic pattern was observed when we estimated models with the 1992 math data (where we could get closest to the set of predictors we used for all the 1990 models).

12 McGranahan and Ghelfi (1991); Teixeira and Mishel (1991, 1992).

13 See Murnane and Levy (1997) and Chapter 7 of this volume.

REFERENCES

Butler, Margaret A. and Calvin L. Beale. 1994. *Rural-Urban Continuum Codes for Metro and Nonmetro Counties, 1993*, USDA-ERS-RED, Washington, DC, September.

Ghelfi, Linda M. And Timothy S. Parker. 1997. "A County-Level Measure of Urban Influence." Rural Economy Division, Economic Research Service, U.S. Department of Agriculture. Staff Paper No. 9702.

Greenberg, Elizabeth J., Paul L. Swaim, and Ruy Teixeira. 1993. "Can Rural Workers Compete for the Jobs of the Future?" In *Agriculture's Changing Horizon: Outlook '93 Proceedings*. Washington, DC: U.S. Department of Agriculture, pp. 919–30.

McGranahan, David A. and Linda M. Ghelfi. 1991. "The Education Crisis and Rural Stagnation in the 1980's." In *Education and Rural Development: Rural Strategies for the 1990's*, edited by Richard W. Long. Washington, DC: Economic Research Service, U.S. Department of Agriculture.

Mishel, Lawrence R. and Ruy Teixeira. 1991. "The Myth of the Coming Labor Shortage: Jobs, Skills and Incomes of America's Workforce 2000." Washington, DC: Economic Policy Institute.

Murnane, Richard J. and Frank Levy. 1997. Teaching the New Basic Skills: Principles for Educating Children to Thrive in a Changing Economy. New York: Free Press.

Stern, Joyce. 1994. "The Condition of Education in Rural Schools." Washington, DC: Office of Educational Research and Improvement, U.S. Department of Education.

Swanson, Linda, ed. 1996. *Racial/Ethnic Minorities in Rural Areas: Progress and Stagnation, 1980–90*. Washington, DC: Economic Research Service, U.S. Department of Agriculture.

Teixeira, Ruy. 1995. "Rural Education and Training: Myths and Misconceptions Dispelled." In *The American Countryside: Rural People and Places*, edited by Emory N. Castle. Lawrence: University Press of Kansas.

Teixeira, Ruy and Lawrence Mishel. 1991. "Upgrading Workers' Skills Not Sufficient to Jump-Start Rural Economy." *Rural Development Perspectives* 7, no. 3 (June–September).

_____. 1992. "The Myth of the Coming Labor Shortage in Rural Areas." Washington, DC: Economic Policy Institute.

_____. 1993. "Whose Skills Shortage—Workers or Management?" *Issues in Science and Technology*, Summer.

_____. 1995. "Skills Shortage or Management Shortage?" In *The New Modern Times: Factors Reshaping the World of Work*, edited by D. Bills. Albany, NY: SUNY Press.

CHAPTER 3

RURAL HIGH SCHOOL COMPLETION

by Kathleen M. Paasch and Paul L. Swaim

INTRODUCTION

G raduating from high school is an important stage in the preparation for adult life. Secondary education provides a core of knowledge and competencies that are preconditions for performing well on many jobs. The decline in the inflation-adjusted wages of high school dropouts since the early 1970's is sobering testimony to the increased importance of finishing high school to individuals' economic prospects (Levy and Murnane 1992). The failure to complete high school also affects a variety of nonmarket outcomes (Haveman and Wolfe 1984). Research indicates that the lack of a high school education can lead to a lower investment in one's own children, an increased risk of divorce, less efficient contraceptive use, lower political participation, and higher mortality rates. Dropping out of high school is not simply a problem for the individual, but one for his or her family and community.

In this chapter, we examine the dropout problem in rural high schools during the early 1990's. Our first goal is to provide an overview of which rural youths fail to finish high school and of the factors that account for this outcome. A second goal is to assess differences and commonalities in the dropout problem between rural and more urbanized areas. Finally, we consider the policy implications of our findings.

RECENT TRENDS IN AGGREGATE DROPOUT RATES

In the last several decades, the share of rural youths who drop out of high school has fallen sharply, largely erasing what had been a substantial rural-urban gap in high school graduation rates. According to data from the Current Population Survey, 16.8 percent of rural 16- to 24-year-olds were dropouts in 1975, only a little higher than the 15.7 percent dropout rate in central cities but much higher than the 10.2 percent rate in other—predominantly suburban—metropolitan areas (Figure 3.1). By 1993, the rural dropout rate had fallen to 11.1 percent and was intermediate between the 16.8 percent central city and 9.3 percent suburb rates. The long valid generalization that rural educational attainment lags urban now must be greatly qualified, so far as secondary education is concerned: rural youths are approximately as likely to earn a high school diploma as metro youths, overall, although suburban youths continue to have a lower dropout rate than either rural or central city youths.

The dramatic improvement in rural dropout rates is good news for rural communities and students, but this good news is subject to two important qualifications. First, more than 10 percent of rural high school students still fail to graduate by age 24, and this group may face a rather bleak future. Policies to identify students at risk of school failure and help them to succeed with their studies are of large potential value. Second, the improvement in rural dropout rates does not mean that the rural workforce is now competitive in terms of attracting firms who demand well-educated workers. Much of the adult workforce left school when rural dropout rates exceeded urban, with the result that 29 percent of the rural population age 25 or older are high school dropouts, compared with 20 per-

FIGURE 3.1. Dropout rates for 16- to 24-year-olds by residence

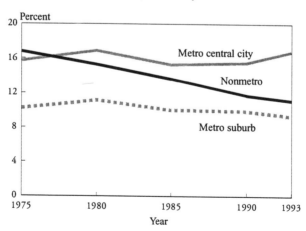

Source: Bureau of the Census, Current Population Reports, Series P-60, various years.

cent of metro adults. Lower dropout rates for new cohorts of rural workers are slowly erasing the rural deficit in secondary education, but progress is slow (see Chapter 8 for a complementary analysis). Also, and as was already noted, the dropout rate in rural schools is still higher than in suburban schools, and this difference may represent a competitive disadvantage for rural areas. Another potential concern is that the quality of rural education might be low or have fallen as more marginal students were retained in the classroom. Greenberg and Teixeira's analysis of achievement test scores provides important evidence that this is not the case (see Chapter 2). Finally, Gibbs' research shows that rural college attendance continues to lag urban, even among new cohorts (see Chapter 4). Despite these caveats, the convergence of rural and urban dropout rates is a social development of great importance.

A FIRST LOOK AT RISK FACTORS

Why have dropout rates remained so high when the individual consequences of dropping out are so negative? Educational researchers have examined this issue in detail, and a number of risk factors increasing the probability of dropping out have been identified (Astone and McLanahan 1991; Natriello 1987). For example, the children of families with incomes below the poverty line, with poorly educated parents, or headed by single mothers are more likely to become dropouts, as are members of certain racial and ethnic minorities. County data from the 1990 Census indicate that children in rural areas are more exposed to certain of these risks than metro children, but less exposed to others (Figure 3.2).

FIGURE 3.2. Share of population with potential risk factors, 1990

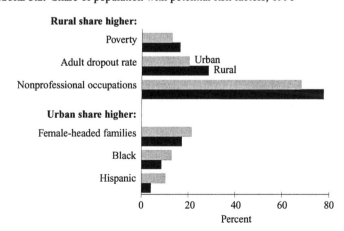

Source: Calculated by the authors using data from the Bureau of the Census.

Rural children are more often poor and more often have parents who are themselves dropouts, but they are less likely to be raised by a single mother or to be black or Hispanic. This initial examination of risk factors for dropping out suggests no easy conclusions about the relative severity of the barriers to raising rural graduation rates, but it does suggest that "at-risk" students in rural schools confront a different mix of potential stumbling blocks than their urban and suburban counterparts.

Community and area characteristics have not received nearly as much attention as demographic and family characteristics in the prior research literature on the causes of dropping out. These "neighborhood" effects may, however, be an important part of the dropout problem and especially salient to understanding how the rural dropout problem differs from the urban. The concept of social capital, as developed by James Coleman (1988), provides a useful theoretical structure for addressing some of these issues. Coleman hypothesizes that children are more likely to conform to social norms, such as completing high school, in communities in which parents' efforts to encourage such behavior are reinforced by other adults who take an active interest in the welfare of the community's children. The greater social cohesion sometimes attributed to rural life suggests that rural communities may tend to possess more such social capital. For example, Ballou and Podgursky's analysis of rural schools suggests that rural education benefits from more effective integration of schooling into the broader life of the community (see Chapter 1).

Characteristics of the local labor market may also have an important influence on the extent of the dropout problem. If few professional and technical jobs are available for local workers, as is the case in most rural labor markets, youths may be less likely to aspire to such careers and, hence, place a lower priority on education. At an economic level, the incentive for rural students to persist in school is reduced because the additional earnings that would follow from more schooling are lower than in urban labor markets, where the demand for well educated workers is greater (see McGranahan and Ghelfi, Chapter 8). The disincentive to invest in education will be mitigated for youths willing to move to areas with better employment opportunities, but some youths may want to remain in their home communities or may be unaware of labor market opportunities elsewhere. Quite apart from rate of return calculations, the scarcity of professional adults in the local community, who can serve as role models, will tend to reduce the number of youths who identify with and aspire to these occupations.[1]

County-level data from the 1990 Census indicate that dropout rates vary quite strongly by the economic specializations of rural counties, which suggests that area differences in labor markets may influence school attainment. Individual-level data are needed, however, to distinguish if labor market incentives directly affect school attainment or if this association operates indirectly through, for example, the impact of the local job mix on family income levels and the share of students living in poverty.

RESEARCH STRATEGY

Our analysis extends prior research in four ways. First, we give particular attention to rural students. Only a few studies using microdata to study dropouts analyze students separately according to urbanicity. Urban, rural, and suburban communities differ by such characteristics as average education level, earnings, employment opportunities, and family structure, and it is likely that the students who drop out of schools in these areas will also differ, not only in terms of the numbers of dropouts but also in terms of processes leading to school failure. Cobb, McIntyre, and Pratt (1989) developed a valuable precursor for this sort of study, but their analysis focuses on the high school senior class of 1980, and their results may not reflect the experience of more recent cohorts of students. Accordingly, a second way our research extends the literature is by analyzing rural high school students in the 1990's. A third limitation of prior research has been a tendency to disregard when a student drops out. That is, it is assumed that the processes that lead younger students to drop out are the same as those influencing older students. We explore this assumption because understanding whether different processes are at work at different ages is important for policy. For example, younger students' decisions whether to persist in school may be more influenced by their families' characteristics, while older students may be more influenced by labor market opportunities. If such differences are substantial, programs geared toward dropout prevention in eleventh grade may provide little in the way of support for potential ninth grade dropouts. The fourth way we go beyond previous research is by expanding the range of covariates considered. In addition to the individual and family factors typically emphasized, we also include several measures of school environment as well as county-level measures of labor market and social conditions. Until recently, such a study would have been impossible to conduct due to the absence of an adequate data set. Happily, such a data set has recently become available to researchers.

DATA

The National Education Longitudinal Study of 1988 (NELS) is comprised of approximately 25,000 eighth-graders surveyed in 1988 with follow-up surveys conducted in 1990 and 1992. NELS is particularly well suited for our study of rural dropouts. The respondents are members of a recent cohort and were initially interviewed in the eighth grade, allowing us to examine "early" dropouts. In addition to student data, NELS contains information gathered from parents, teachers, and school administrators making possible many levels of analysis. Finally, NELS data can be used to compare dropout patterns in rural schools with those in urban and suburban schools, although some complications arise.

The NELS data classify each student according to whether he or she attends a rural, urban, or suburban school. The NELS urbanicity classifications do not correspond exactly to the Bureau of the Census' official designations of rural and urban places or of metropolitan and nonmetropolitan counties, but they appear to characterize urbanicity in a reasonable fashion. In order to verify these classifications and enable us to supplement the NELS data with county-level measures of labor market and social conditions, we received special permission from the Department of Education to attach county identifiers to the data. These county codes indicate that 99.5 percent of students living in a nonmetro county were classified by NELS as attending a rural school, and virtually every student classified by NELS as attending a suburban or urban school lived in a metro county. It should be noted, however, that 17.1 percent of the rural NELS students lived in metro counties, which is probably an accurate reflection of the fact that many metro counties contain areas possessing a rural character. For technical reasons, we were able to obtain county identifiers for only 72 percent of the total NELS sample. Due to this limitation, we conduct most of our empirical analysis using the full sample and the NELS urbanicity codes. When we incorporate county-level information into the analysis, we use the smaller sample.

In order to examine possible differences in the likelihood of dropping out as determined by age, we examine the data in two panels. Panel 1 respondents were selected on the condition of having completed interviews in both 1988 (as eighth-graders) and 1990. Panel 2 respondents had to have been interviewed in 1990 (as tenth-graders) and then again in 1992. In choosing a definition of "dropouts", we follow the procedure suggested by Department of Education documentation: for the period between eighth and tenth grades (panel 1), dropouts were defined as those who reported being absent from school 20 or more consecutive days when contacted by an interviewer in Spring 1990. Other students included in the dropout group were those who had had more than one episode of 20 or more day absences and had been attending school for less than two weeks prior to the first follow-up interview. For the period between tenth and twelfth grades (panel 2), dropouts were those who were attending tenth grade at the time of the 1990 interview but were neither graduates nor regularly attending school when contacted for the Spring 1992 interview. Some of the students we classify as dropouts no doubt will eventually earn a high school diploma or GED. The term dropout, as used here, is really shorthand for not progressing in a steady manner toward graduation, and hence being at substantial risk of never finishing high school.

We were initially concerned there would be too few dropouts between eighth and tenth grades to support our statistical analysis, because the legal age to leave school is 16 in most states, but dropping out during the early years of high school is not as uncommon an occurrence as might be expected. Many early dropouts have been held back for one or more grades making them legally old enough to leave school. Others appear simply to have left school at early ages. Similar percentages dropped out between eighth and tenth grades (panel 1) and between tenth and twelfth grades (panel 2).

Sample sizes and dropout rates for panels 1 and 2 are presented in Table 3.1.

TABLE 3.1. Sample sizes and dropout rates[a]

Item	United States	Rural	Urban	Suburban
Younger students, 8th-10th grades, 1988-90 (Panel 1):				
Sample size	17,424	5,576	4,495	7,353
Dropout rate	6.0	6.3	7.7	4.8
Older students, 10th-12th grades, 1990-92 (Panel 2):				
Sample size	16,749	5,285	4,653	6,811
Dropout rate	6.7	8.1	6.6	5.5

[a]See text for definition of dropouts.
Source: Calculated by authors using data from the National Education Longitudinal Survey.

FIGURE 3.3. Dropout rates among students by age and risk factors

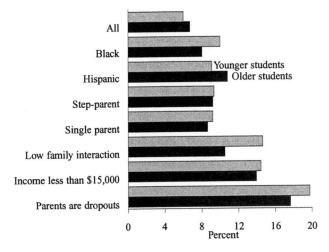

Source: Calculated by the authors using data from the National Education Longitudinal Survey.

Dropout rates for the full NELS sample are 6.0 and 6.7 percent. The corresponding rates for rural students are a little higher in panel 1 at 6.3 percent and quite a bit higher in panel 2 at 8.1 percent. Suburban dropout rates are the lowest in both panels, while rural and urban dropout rates are fairly similar although the rural dropouts are more concentrated in the tenth–twelfth grade period.

The NELS data confirm that minorities and children from low-resource families have above-average dropout rates (Figure 3.3). Dropout rates also differ when students are classified by many other variables available in the NELS data, but we would like to analyze which of these associations reflect the most important causal relationships. Multivariate statistical techniques are required to judge better the independent effects of these personal and other factors on the odds of dropping out, and we now turn to such an analysis.

MULTIVARIATE ANALYSIS OF THE DETERMINANTS OF DROPPING OUT

Basic Logit Model

Dropping out of high school is the result of a complex array of causes, and multivariate regression is an indispensable tool for sorting out the relative importance of the various factors involved. We adopt a logit model, which is a widely used modification of standard regression techniques for cases when the dependent variable is a discrete event, such as dropping out of high school, and the analysis focuses on modeling how various factors influence the probability that event actually occurs. Unlike simple tabulations, the logit coefficients for these variables provide estimates of each factor's independent effect on the probability of dropping out, holding all of the other factors constant.

For our independent variables, we selected 17 individual, family, school, and community variables that are available in the NELS and are either risk factors potentially leading to increased dropping out or resources potentially helping students to persevere in high school. We include dummy variables for whether the student is black, is of another nonwhite race, is Hispanic, is female, lives in the South, lives with a step-parent, lives with a single parent, has parents who do not know the student's friends, lives in a rural community, or lives in an urban community. We also include variables measuring the number of siblings and the number of times the student has changed schools. Three variables measuring the characteristics of the student's eighth grade school are also included: the percent of the students who are white, the percent receiving free lunches, and the attendance rate.

The final two independent variables require a little more explanation. Family socioeconomic status (SES) is a composite measure of family income and parents' education and occupation. Parent-child interaction is a composite measure of interactions that is constructed from seven separate questions about the breadth, depth, and frequency of interactions.

When we could identify the student's county of residence, we added a large number of variables measuring county economic and social conditions to our analysis file. Most of these measures were taken from the Summary Tape File (STF-3) for the 1990 Census of Population. We also added some labor market variables from the Current Population Survey.

Basic Logit Results

The estimated coefficients in a logit model are a little more difficult to interpret than are the more familiar standard regression coefficients. The key to interpretation is to think in terms of the effect of an independent variable on the odds ratio of the event happening, where the odds ratio is defined as the ratio of the probability the event happens to the probability of it not happening.[2] Consider dropout rates. If a student has a 10 percent chance of dropping out, the corresponding odds ratio is 10 percent divided by 90 percent, or one-ninth. The effect of an increase in an independent variable can be expressed as its multiplicative effect on the odds ratio. Suppose we consider a second student who is the same in every respect except that he or she lives with a step-parent. If the logit coefficient indicates a multiplicative effect of 1.0, then living with a step-parent has no effect on the chances of dropping out. A multiplicative effect greater than 1.0 indicates increased chances of dropping out and an effect less than 1.0 a decreasd chance.

The fourth column of Table 3.2 reports our logit estimates of the effects of a unit increase in each of the 17 independent variables on the odds ratio for dropping out. For example, the .326 value for SES in panel 1 indicates that the dropout odds for an eighth grade student with an SES score one unit above a reference student's score is only .326 times (about a third of) that of the reference student.

Some of the variables that alone are strongly associated with above-average dropout rates turn out to have no significant effect when we control for the effects of other variables. For example, once we control for family and school characteristics, black and Hispanic students are not more likely to drop out than non-Hispanic whites; indeed they appear slightly less likely to drop out. Of particular importance for our analysis, rural and urban residences also lose their significance, suggesting that the schooling advantages of suburban students are adequately captured by the other independent variables. This does not mean that minority or rural students do not have above-average dropout rates, but that their higher dropout rates are due to their greater exposure to some of the risk factors, such as low family SES, that are controlled for in the model. In a following section, we analyze in some detail which differences in risk exposures tend to raise or lower rural dropout rates.

Variables that significantly increase the risk of dropping out for one or both panels of students include living in the South, low SES, living with a step-parent, limited interactions with parents, parents not knowing student's friends, frequently changing schools, and attending a school with a large minority enrollment. These findings are all in accordance with our expectations based on earlier studies. In particular, our analysis strongly confirms that students whose families have adequate economic resources and whose parents are actively engaged

TABLE 3.2.   Logit analysis of the effects of risk factors and resources on dropout rates by residence

				Panel 1: younger students, 8th-10th grades, 1988-90		
				Logit model estimate of change in the risk of dropping out	Change in rural dropout risk from changing rural mean to the mean for--	
		Data means			Urban	Suburban
Variable	Rural	Urban	Suburban		students	students
		Average			*Multiplicative effect on the odds ratio*	
Black (yes = 1)	.080	.245	.081	.864	NS	NS
Hispanic (yes = 1)	.063	.166	.082	.726	NS	NS
Other nonwhite (yes = 1)	.026	.066	.050	.519*	.974	.985
Female (yes = 1)	.497	.510	.494	.915	NS	NS
South (yes = 1)	.407	.426	.272	1.532***	1.008	.994
SES (-2.97 - 2.56)	-.279	-.108	.051	.326***	.825	.691
Step-parent (yes = 1)	.153	.138	.150	1.361*	.995	.999
Single-parent (yes = 1)	.157	.228	.147	1.063	NS	NS
Number of siblings	1.291	1.265	1.276	.846**	1.004	1.003
Parent-child interaction (1 - 3.5)	2.657	2.709	2.713	.564***	.974	.968
Parents do not know friends (yes = 1)	.077	.095	.062	1.464*	1.010	.994
Times changed school	1.017	1.328	1.145	1.462***	1.125	1.050
White enrollment in school (%)	4.569	3.425	4.514	.867**	1.021	1.008
Free lunch receipt in school (%)	1.909	1.771	1.389	.809**	1.020	1.116
School attendance (%)	94.2	92.8	94.1	.939***	1.084	.998
Rural (yes = 1)	1	0	0	.972	NS	NS
Urban (yes = 1)	0	1	0	1.133	NS	NS
Model chi-square (df)	NA	NA	NA	1421.3 (19)	NA	NA
Sample size	NA	NA	NA	16,304	NA	NA
Total compositional effect on the relative rural dropout odds ratio	NA	NA	NA	NA	1.009	.730

See notes at end of table.   --Continued

TABLE 3.2. Logit analysis of the effects of risk factors and resources on dropout rates by residence--Continued

	Panel 2: older students, 10-12th grades, 1990-92					
				Logit model estimate of change in the risk of dropping out	Change in rural dropout risk from changing rural mean to the mean for--	
	Data means				Urban students	Suburban students
Variable	Rural	Urban	Suburban			
		Average			*Multiplicative effect on the odds ratio*	
Black (yes = 1)	.064	.182	.059	.667 *	.953	1.002
Hispanic (yes = 1)	.059	.139	.060	.822	NS	NS
Other nonwhite (yes = 1)	.025	.067	.051	.783	NS	NS
Female (ye s = 1)	.498	.519	.491	1.057	NS	NS
South (yes = 1)	.371	.363	.272	1.031	NS	NS
SES (-2.97 - 2.56)	-.162	.086	.190	.407**	.800	.729
Step-parent (yes = 1)	.132	.129	.142	1.476**	.997	1.004
Single-parent (yes = 1)	.138	.159	.138	1.204	NS	NS
Number of siblings	1.815	1.779	1.738	1.200**	.993	.986
Parent-child interaction (1 - 3.5)	2.343	2.393	2.429	.769***	.987	.978
Parents do not know friends (yes = 1)	.065	.063	.049	1.032	NS	NS
Times changed school	1.017	1.282	1.199	1.185***	1.045	1.031
White enrollment in school (%)	4.167	3.254	4.167	.895*	1.017	1.000
Free lunch receipt in school (%)	1.858	1.474	1.346	1.078	NS	NS
School attendance (%)	93.4	92.1	93.0	1.009	NS	NS
Rural (yes = 1)	1	0	0	1.190	NS	NS
Urban (yes = 1)	0	1	0	.951	NS	NS
Model chi-square (df)	NA	NA	NA	898.0 (24)	NA	NA
Sample size	NA	NA	NA	15,916	NA	NA
Total compositional effect on the relative rural dropout odds ratio	NA	NA	NA	NA	.793	.723

NA = Not applicable.

NS = Associated logit coefficient not statistically significant.

Note: ***,**,* denote statistical significance at 1, 5, and 10 percent confidence levels, respectively.

Source: Calculated by authors using data from the National Education Longitudinal Survey.

in their lives are much less likely to experience school failure. The great importance of these family characteristics also suggests that it may be difficult for schools to offset the disadvantages faced by students lacking these resources.

Some of our other results are more difficult to interpret and—while offering some interesting insights—indicate a need for further research. For the younger—but not the older—students, it appears schools with good attendance rates or many students receiving free lunches are more successful at graduating their students. It seems reasonable that student attendance would be higher in schools offering a good learning environment, but the school lunch finding seems less reasonable and should be treated cautiously. We included the school lunch variable as a proxy for the prevalence of poverty among the student body and expected dropout rates to rise, rather than fall, with this variable due to a negative peer group effect from concentrated poverty. A possible, but speculative, explanation for the opposite result is that students whose incomes are high compared with their peers' incomes may do better in school. Holding family income constant (as our logit model does), a student's relative income in the school is higher, the higher the share of other students who are poor.

Contrary to our expectations, older students' probabilities of dropping out are just as influenced by family variables as are the dropout probabilities for younger students. Parent-child interactions diminish between eighth and tenth grades, reflecting increasing independence with age, but both age groups' school prospects strongly reflect conditions in their families. We also expected the dropout probability to be higher for students with more siblings, because they would receive less attention from their parents. This was the case in the older group but not in the younger. We lack a satisfactory explanation for this result but conjecture that older students in large families might face greater pressures to help with child care or to earn money.

Our results provide no support for the prediction that higher social capital in rural communities enhances the educational outcomes of rural students. We did not include a direct measure of social capital among the model's independent variables, because the NELS data do not contain a reliable measure of this rather elusive concept. Nonetheless, if rural communities benefit from an important social capital advantage, the rural residence variable should have picked up that advantage, which was not the case. An important task for future researchers, perhaps especially for those using ethnographic techniques, is to develop direct measures of social capital and its effects.

Adding County-Level Variables to the Model

For the subsample of students for whom we could determine county of residence, we added an extensive list of county-level measures of labor market and other economic and social conditions to the list of independent variables supplied with the NELS. When added to the logit regression model, the county-level variables typically were not statistically significant although there were a few exceptions among the labor market variables (discussed below). The insignificance of most county-level variables does not mean that community characteristics do not matter for school success. For example, labor market conditions clearly affect dropout rates indirectly, by first affecting family income levels and parents' occupations. Although we find no evidence for an additional, direct effect it may be that county boundaries do not adequately capture the relevant neighborhoods within which these area effects operate. For example, in some areas the local labor market may embrace several counties and in others only a small part of the county of residence.

The few cases in which labor market variables explained a significant share of differences in the likelihood of dropping out were mostly limited to older students; this is consistent with our expectation that older students are more strongly affected by labor market conditions than younger. The labor market characteristic that appears to have the largest direct impact on lowering dropout rates is a relative abundance of midlevel jobs that do not require a college education. Contrary to our expectations, the availability of professional-level jobs does not appear to be salient to potential dropouts, except as it operates through family SES. This may be because the relevant alternative to dropping out for a struggling student is unlikely to be a professional degree. What matters is whether the local labor market offers a substantial number of medium-skilled jobs that a high school graduate can better compete for than a dropout. The availability of professional jobs may matter much more for college attendance and the migration choices frequently associated with higher education (see Gibbs, Chapter 4).

Which Factors Most Disadvantage Rural Students?

Our logit regressions provide quantitative estimates of the impacts of various risk factors on students' odds of successfully graduating. By combining these findings with data on the differential exposure of rural students to these risk factors, as compared with urban and suburban students, we can assess the risk factors that play especially large roles in the rural dropout problem and hence require special attention in rural educational and dropout prevention programs.

On average, rural, urban, and suburban students differ substantially on many of the factors potentially affecting dropping out of school, which we included in our logit regression (Table 3.2, columns one through three). For example, the family socioeconomic status (SES) average is considerably lower for rural than urban students, who in turn have lower SES than suburban students. We calculated how the risk of dropping out would change for rural students if their mean value for that independent variable were changed to the urban (column five) or suburban (column six) mean values. As before, the change in dropout risk is expressed in terms of the multiplicative effect on the odds ratio. For example, the average rural student in the younger age group would be only .825 times as likely to drop out if his or her SES level increased to the average metro SES level and only .691 times as likely to drop out at the average suburban SES level. The corresponding values for an average older rural student are .800 and .729.

Lower rural SES is the single largest factor elevating rural dropout rates relative to urban and suburban rates, but several other factors also advantage or disadvantage rural students. For example, the Waltons notwithstanding, rural dropout rates are also elevated by lower parent-child interaction than in urban and suburban families. On a more positive note, rural dropout rates are lowered because rural students less frequently experience the dislocation of changing schools.[3] Other variables have smaller effects, or effects that vary depending on the age group considered or whether rural students are compared with urban or suburban students.

The total compositional effects indicate that rural dropout rates are raised quite strongly relative to suburban rates by differences in the independent variables for both the younger and the older students (Table 3.2, bottom row). The corresponding odds ratios (.730 and .723) are similar in magnitude to those implied by the rural and suburban dropout rates reported in Table 3.1, indicating that our logit model does a good job of accounting for the excess of rural over suburban dropouts. The results for the rural/urban comparison are somewhat different. The total compositional differences between rural and urban students do a good job of explaining why the rural dropout rate is higher for the older students, but they explain very little of the excess of the urban dropout rate for younger students.

EDUCATIONAL AND OCCUPATIONAL ASPIRATIONS

The educational and occupational aspirations of rural, urban, and suburban students can help to make sense of these dropout patterns. In choosing to dropout, students are making an important decision about their futures. We would expect that their career aspirations and the role they envision for schooling in realizing those aspirations is a key factor in making that choice. In this context, proponents of educational reform recently have emphasized the need to better manage the school-to-work transition. Under the current "nonsystem" it appears that many noncollege-bound high school students see little relationship between their class work and their future career prospects and, hence, exert little effort in school. Comparisons with secondary schools in Germany, Japan, and elsewhere have motivated proposals to strengthen the ties between high schools and surrounding employers. The federal Educational Reform Act of 1994 moves in this direction by supporting youth apprenticeship programs that integrate work experience and vocational preparation with high school study, but provides few resources for achieving these goals. Local initiatives by employers and schools, such as the Boston Compact, have also pioneered closer links between high schools and the world of work.

The NELS data indicate that students have quite high occupational aspirations, which have risen over time and appear to be overly optimistic in comparison with the mix of jobs that will be available (Table 3.3). When they were in the eighth grade, 52 percent of rural students expected to be employed in managerial, professional, or technical occupations at age 30. The percentage of students aspiring to those jobs rose steadily over the following four years, with 64 percent aspiring to them in their senior year. To some extent, this rise reflects the tendency of dropouts to have lower aspirations, but most of the rise reflects upward adjustments on the part of continuing students.

Compared with urban and suburban students, however, rural students were not very ambitious. Urban and suburban students were even more likely than rural students to expect to hold the best-paying and highest-status jobs. Compared with opportunities to work in those fields, however, all students appear to be overly optimistic. While about two-thirds of high school seniors aspire to managerial, professional, and technical jobs, less than a quarter of rural jobs and only a third

TABLE 3.3. Type of work expected at age 30 compared with occupational mix of employment

Group	Managerial, professional, or technical job	Craft or operative job
	Percent	
Type of work expected by:		
1988 eighth-graders		
Rural	51.6	7.6
Urban	59.0	5.0
Suburban	58.3	5.0
1990 tenth-graders		
Rural	61.3	8.7
Urban	70.2	5.8
Suburban	69.3	2.9
1992 twelfth-graders		
Rural	63.5	6.2
Urban	74.1	3.1
Suburban	71.2	4.2
1980 twelfth-graders		
Rural	50.8	13.2
Nonrural	65.1	7.8
Occupational mix of employment:		
1980		
Nonmetro	19.9	32.3
Metro	27.4	25.1
1990		
Nonmetro	22.6	29.0
Metro	32.0	20.5

Source: Jobs expected by students in 1988, 1990, and 1992 calculated by the authors using data from the National Education Longitudinal Survey; jobs expected by students in 1980 from Cobb, McIntyre, and Pratt (1989); and occupational mix calculated by the authors using data from the 1980 and 1990 Censuses of Population.

of metro jobs were in those occupations in 1990. The other side of the coin is that fewer students aspire to craft and operative jobs than are available. This suggests a possible disconnection between school and work, particularly for students lacking a strong aptitude for advanced academic training. It also appears that this disconnection may have increased in recent years. High school seniors in 1980 were considerably less likely than 1992 seniors to aspire to professional jobs and more likely to aspire to the best blue-collar jobs. While employment opportunities have declined, at least relatively, for many nonprofessional occupations, students may be over-reacting to this trend.

Students' educational plans can be used to paint a similar picture (Table 3.4). Rural students are less ambitious than urban and suburban students, particularly as regards post-graduate studies. However, a large majority of students in all three areas anticipate continuing their educations beyond high school (consistent with their occupational aspirations). By the time they were seniors, only one student in ten anticipated no postsecondary education, and over half anticipated earning at least a bachelor's degree. Seniors in 1980 were considerably less ambitious, a clear indication that high school students are now aware that advanced education is increasingly decisive in determining who gets ahead but may also be unaware of potentially attractive career options that do not require advanced degrees.

Unrealistic or not, students' aspirations appear to influence schooling outcomes. Dropout rates are much higher for students with low educational and occupational aspirations (Figure 3.4). Students who aspire to professional occupations and the education levels those occupations require are more likely to persist in their schooling. Policies to raise the aspirations levels of rural students sometimes may be a valuable component of dropout prevention programs. The fact that urban students have higher aspirations than rural students, yet drop out at comparable rates, indicates that higher aspirations alone are not sufficient to guarantee schooling success. The greater need may be to develop more effective pathways from high schools into careers for youths who are unlikely to pursue advanced academic training.

CONCLUSION

The dropout rate for rural youths fell sharply between 1975 and 1993, closing the rural-metro gap in high school completion, but only narrowing the rural-suburban gap. Despite these gains, more than 10 percent of rural youths still do not finish high school and probably face bleak employment prospects. We find that the effects of individual, family, community, and school risk factors on the probability of dropping out are similar for rural, suburban, and urban students, but the fraction of students exposed to these risks differs significantly across the three community types. Low parental education and family income appear to be the biggest barriers to reducing rural dropout rates. Low parent-child interaction also

TABLE 3.4. Students' educational expectations by grade and residence

Group	Won't finish high school	High school graduate	Vocational technical school	Some college	B.A. or B.S.	M.A. or more
			Percent			
1988 eighth-graders:						
Rural	2.0	13.9	11.3	13.5	40.7	18.7
Urban	1.5	8.8	8.6	14.0	41.7	25.4
Suburban	1.7	9.1	8.5	12.4	44.8	24.0
1990 tenth-graders:						
Rural	2.6	15.1	16.2	17.0	28.0	21.1
Urban	1.9	10.0	11.9	16.4	30.1	29.7
Suburban	1.5	9.3	11.8	18.6	32.3	26.5
1992 twelfth-graders:						
Rural	0.3	9.5	17.3	17.1	36.9	18.9
Urban	0.3	4.5	8.7	12.7	38.1	35.8
Suburban	0.1	5.1	11.1	15.7	35.7	32.2
1980 twelfth-graders:						
Rural	0.8	22.8	23.0	15.4	22.6	13.3
Urban	0.7	14.1	17.7	15.5	26.1	26.0
Suburban	0.3	13.7	16.7	15.4	27.8	26.0

Source: Students' educational expectations in 1988, 1990, and 1992 calculated by the authors using data from the National Education Longitudinal Survey; students' educational expectations in 1980 from Cobb, McIntyre, and Pratt (1989).

FIGURE 3.4. Dropout rates for eighth-graders by expectations

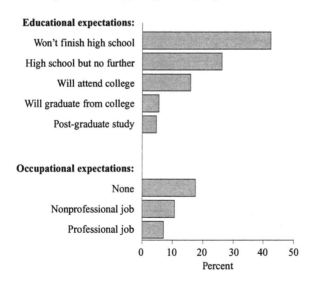

Source: Calculated by the authors using data from the National Education Longitudinal Survey.

elevated rural dropout rates, but less frequent school changes lowered the rural rate. The fact that many of the most important causes of school failure appear to be rooted in family circumstances suggests the difficulty of developing effective remedies, especially at a time when economic and demographic trends are eroding the position of economically marginal workers and increasing family income inequality (Karoly and Burtless 1995). It is unrealistic to expect rural high schools alone to develop an adequate response to the rural dropout problem.

Our results also indicate that the process of dropping out begins early in high school for many students but that the factors causing school failure are quite similar for younger and older students. Larger numbers of siblings and adverse labor market conditions appear to adversely affect students only in the last two years of high school, which suggests that policies aimed at dropout prevention should be alert to potential strains faced by older students in balancing school with family responsibilities and work.[4]

Somewhat more speculatively, our analysis of students' educational and occupational aspirations suggests that a significant disconnection between schools and labor markets may have developed. Students appear to be acutely aware that the economy has shifted away from blue-collar jobs and that the best paying jobs are those requiring four or more years of college study, but they may be overreacting to these trends. The fact that almost all students planning for a career are planning for a professional career suggests that students today have little belief that other careers are viable. This finding reinforces recent concerns that the school-to-work transition for noncollege-bound students is increasingly dysfunctional. The disconnection between schooling and nonprofessional careers appears to be no more severe in rural areas, but it may matter more in those areas, because a larger percentage of rural workers hold nonprofessional jobs. This disconnection also suggests that youth apprenticeships and similar initiatives, intended to better link secondary schooling and work for nonbaccalaureate-bound students, may deserve higher priority.

NOTES

1 Human capital theory (Becker 1984) emphasizes the rate of return to education as the key determinant of educational attainment. The broader approach adopted here also incorporates sociological factors that may influence the extent to which youths' educational choices actually reflect the purposive pursuit of their long-run economic interests.

2 If P denotes the probability a student drops out of high school, then $R = [P/(1-P)]$ is the odds ratio of dropping out. The logit model is defined by the assumption that $\ln(R) = X$. That is, the natural logarithm of the odds ratio is assumed to be linearly related to a vector of independent variables (X). Maximum likelihood estimates of the logit coefficients are easily calculated.

3 The fact that rural students change schools less often is suggestive of more stable school-community ties that may represent a form of social capital (see Ballou and Podgursky, Chapter 1). However, the logit coefficient on the number of school changes

captures an individual- rather than community-level effect.

4 Earlier research suggests that some mixing of employment and high school may actually improve a student's odds of graduating but that working too many hours increases the risk of dropping out (Swaim 1994). It may be that some exposure to the labor market helps students to better appreciate the economic payoff to persisting in their studies.

REFERENCES

Astone, Nan Marie and Sara S. McLanahan. 1991. "Family Structure, Parental Practices and High School Completion." *American Sociological Review* 56:309–20.

Becker, Gary S. 1984. *Human Capital*, 2d ed. New York: Columbia University Press.

Cobb, Robert A., W.G. McIntyre, and P.A. Pratt. 1989. "Vocational and Educational Aspirations of High School Students: A Problem for Rural America." *Research in Rural Education* 6(2):11–16.

Coleman, James. 1988. "Social Capital in the Creation of Human Capital." *American Journal of Sociology* 94(S):95–120.

Haveman, Robert H. and Barbara Wolfe. 1984. "Schooling and Economic Well-Being: The Role of Nonmarket Effects." *Journal of Human Resources* 19(3):377–407.

Karoly, Lynn A. and Gary Burtless. 1995. "Demographic Change, Rising Earnings Inequality, and the Distribution of Personal Well-Being, 1959–1989." *Demography* 32(3):379–405.

Levy, Frank and Richard J. Murnane. 1992. "U.S. Earnings Levels and Earnings Inequality: A Review of Recent Trends and Proposed Explanations." *Journal of Economic Literature* 30(3):1333–81.

Natriello, Gary (ed.). 1987. *School Dropouts: Patterns and Policies*. New York: Teachers College Press.

Swaim, Paul. 1994. Work Experience, Local Labor Markets, and Dropping out of High School. In *American Statistical Association 1994 Proceedings of the Social Statistics Section*, pp. 207–12.

U.S. Department of Commerce. Bureau of the Census. Various years. *Current Population Reports*, Series P-60.

CHAPTER 4

COLLEGE COMPLETION AND RETURN MIGRATION AMONG RURAL YOUTH

by Robert M. Gibbs

INTRODUCTION

G oing off to college is often a decisive event in a person's life course. College opens the door to a world of expanded opportunity, of rewarding careers, and of stable, livable earnings. For rural high school graduates, more so than urban, the decision to attend college commits them to making choices about whether to leave home and, if so, whether to return. Despite the potential rewards, rural students face more obstacles getting to college and have more trouble reaping the benefits if they choose to come home. Undoubtedly this explains in part why the proportion of rural adults with college degrees grew more slowly than that among urban adults during the 1980's (a 2 percent rise versus 5 percent), even though average years of schooling were converging.

For many rural places, the loss of young adults who attend college is the primary agent of human capital change. Indeed, for rural counties the connection between education and migration presents a dilemma: do they educate their children well, only to have them leave? Earlier chapters in this volume have uncovered many positive qualities of rural schools. Teachers are often more satisfied with their work environment than their urban counterparts, class sizes are smaller, extracurricular problems are fewer—and students seem to perform as well in the countryside as in the city. But if high achievers from good schools are more likely to go away to college, the best efforts of jurisdictions to improve local labor quality through education policies are compromised. Contrarily, if achievement is less likely to be extended to further education, rural individuals suffer diminished prospects.

My purpose in this chapter is to answer two related sets of questions. First, what are the characteristics of rural people and places that make rural high school graduates less likely to become college graduates and graduates less likely to return home? Second, how does migration related to college attendance and return redistribute human capital geographically? The answers lie at the center of the rural workforce quality issue. The distinctive social and economic characteristics of rural areas determined largely by existing job and human capital structures help perpetuate lower college attendance and return rates in an ongoing cycle. Along with the definitional lack of geographic access to colleges, these features complicate attempts to improve the rural workforce.

ABOUT THE DATA

The National Longitudinal Survey of Youth (NLSY), a project of the Center for Human Resource Research at Ohio State University, tracks the annual work, education, and migration experiences of over 12,000 young people who were 14 to 21 years old by 1979. Approximately 3,000 of these comprised a supplemental military sample that was discontinued after 1984, leaving over 9,000 to be followed through 1991. Blacks and those in poverty are sampled in disproportionately large numbers to allow reasonably detailed analyses of these groups.

In the initial interview, respondents were asked a set of background questions about themselves and their families, including residence at birth and at age 14. The NLSY's advantages for this study lie in its large sample of youth at a period of key school and work choices and its annual responses about these choices, along with county of residence. Although its timing makes it the least current data set used in this book, the rich detail available allows statistical analysis of a great variety of research issues.[1]

HOW URBAN AND RURAL
COLLEGE ATTAINMENT RATES COMPARE

Earlier in this century, college graduates were much less common in rural areas than in urban. Education levels no doubt reflected the rigid urban-rural hierarchy of occupations, with high-wage nonfarm jobs clustered in cities. Our primary record of this separation of status has been decennial censuses, which generally refer to the entire adult population. Over time, the proportion of the rural population with college degrees has risen, and until the 1980's was slowly converging with urban levels.

For our purposes, however, a conventional measure of overall regional education attainment masks its two components, the rate for natives and the rate for immigrants. In the NLSY, each respondent is asked his or her county of residence at age 14. This information allows us to separate the components and to compare attainment rates for individuals who grew up in rural and urban environments (Table 4.1). Consistent with the notion that the distribution of workers across space reflects the distribution of skill demand, the urban-rural college completion gap is smaller when metro status is identified before college. The difference is 8 points for respondents whose status is measured at age 25, but this drops to 4 points when status is measured at age 14.

The proportions in Table 4.1 are independent of one another. Yet the likelihood that a person completes college can be understood as the product of a succession of events, each conditional upon previous decisions. The college graduate must first acquire a high school diploma, then decide to attend college, and then complete a program of study. These decisions are determined by personal attributes

TABLE 4.1. Educational attainment rates at age 25 by gender, race, and region, 1982-89

Residence and education attained	Total	Men	Women	Blacks	Whites	Southern whites
			Percent			
Rural						
Graduated from high school	85	83	86	75	86	79
Went on to college	48	45	50	35	49	40
Graduated from a 2- or 4-year program	25	24	26	15	26	21
Graduated from a 4-year program	19	19	18	12	20	17
Graduated from a 2- or 4-year program by residence at age 25	22	20	24	9	24	22
Urban						
Graduated from high school	86	84	87	78	87	84
Went on to college	56	51	57	48	57	58
Graduated from a 2- or 4-year program	29	27	29	16	32	32
Graduated from a 4-year program	23	22	22	11	25	25
Graduated from a 2- or 4-year program by residence at age 25	30	30	30	17	32	32

Note: Young adults were ages 14 to 21 in 1978. Rural and urban status are defined by residence at age 14, unless noted otherwise.

Source: Calculated by the author using data from the 1991 National Longitudinal Survey of Youth.

and preferences as well as by family, labor market, and societal forces. Understanding why rural young adults have lower college graduation rates, then, requires looking at urban-rural differences at each schooling transition decision. Rural and urban young people are equally likely to graduate from high school, with about 85 percent of each group acquiring diplomas or GEDs (Table 4.2). Differences emerge, however, at the point of college attendance; 65 percent of urban high school graduates reported attending college, including community colleges, compared with 56 percent of rural respondents. This gap essentially disappears at the next level. Among college attenders, urban and rural students are equally likely to finish their college programs, with rural students slightly ahead of urban in completing any degree (including two-year programs) and urban students slightly ahead of rural students in completing 4-year degrees.

These patterns are consistent for men, women, and whites. Within each group, rural and urban students are equally likely to be high school graduates, but rural students are significantly less likely to attend college. Among those who attend,

TABLE 4.2. Conditional educational attainment rates for young adults by gender, race, and region, 1982-89

Residence and education attained	Total	Men	Women	Blacks	Whites	Southern whites
			Percent			
Rural						
Graduated from high school	85	83	86	75	86	79
Went on to college	56	54	58	47	57	56
Graduated from a 2- or 4-year program	53	54	52	43	54	54
Graduated from a 4-year program	39	42	37	33	40	44
Urban						
Graduated from high school	86	84	87	78	87	84
Went on to college	65	64	66	62	66	69
Graduated from a 2- or 4-year program	52	53	51	34	55	55
Graduated from a 4-year program	41	43	39	22	44	43

Note: Young adults were ages 14 to 21 in 1978. The reported percentages are based on the number of young adults who attained the preceding education level. Rural and urban status are defined by residence at age 14, unless noted otherwise.

Source: Calculated by the author using data from the 1991 National Longitudinal Survey of Youth.

graduation rates are virtually identical. The story is different for blacks, whose attainment rates at all stages fall well below whites'. Rural blacks' college attendance rate is much lower than their urban counterparts' rate, but rural black attenders complete a college program, whether 2-year or 4-year, much more often than urban black attenders. Lower family incomes, lower parental educational attainment, and, for many, coming from persistently poor areas undoubtedly provide fewer resources and less incentive for rural blacks to go to college. But once there, their motivation to follow through is greater, a finding obscured in conventional attainment tables.

Being rural and black overwhelmingly means being southern (just over 90 percent of nonmetro blacks lived in the South in 1990). Previous chapters in this volume document the southern disadvantage in education achievement and dropout rates. We might expect, then, that region also explains a portion of the disparity between rural blacks and other groups. Comparisons among blacks, all whites, and southern whites help reveal the regional effect on college attainment. Rural southern whites graduate from high school at a rate similar to that of urban blacks, that is, more frequently than rural blacks but less frequently than urban whites. At this level of education, being in the rural South and being black appear to be equally disadvantageous. But college attendance and graduation rates are indistinguishable for rural southern and all whites, while both rural and urban blacks are much less likely than whites to attend or graduate. Region, then, figures prominently in high school, but not college, attainment, while race figures in both.

In Table 4.1, migration flows between urban and rural areas explained about half the difference in college completion for 25-year-olds. The remaining difference is due to educational attainment levels, whose probabilities can be decomposed into a set of factors indexed to sum to 100 percent. The index for each stage of education indicates its relative contribution to the final difference in the urban-rural college graduation rate for this age group (Table 4.3).[2] A positive number indicates that the event favors the urban population, while a negative number indicates a rural advantage. Since the numbers can have opposite signs, it is possible for any given number to be larger than 100.

The top panel shows the decomposition when college is defined as two- or four-year; it highlights the importance of college attendance in the final urban-rural difference. Attendance explains nearly all of the total gap related to education choice for the total youth population. The greatest difference among subgroups is between whites and blacks: attendance explains only 75 percent of the gap for whites but over 300 percent for blacks. Without higher graduation rates (conditional on attendance) for rural blacks, urban-rural differences would be much greater. In the bottom panel, college attendance refers only to four-year schools. The gap attributable to attendance is lower, although it is the still the single most important factor. Unlike the pattern for all types of college, conditional college graduation from a senior college or university favors urban students. Less advanced preparation and greater distance from home may explain why rural

TABLE 4.3. Indexed effects of compositional factors on differences in rural-urban college completion

College type and education level	Total	Men	Women	Blacks	Whites
	Percent				
2- or 4-year graduates					
High school graduates	10	11	8	46	9
College attenders	100	96	104	307	75
College graduates	-9	-6	-12	-253	16
Total rural-urban gap	100	100	100	100	100
4-year graduates					
High school graduates	7	9	6	-62	7
College attenders	71	76	69	-411	54
College graduates	22	16	25	573	39
Total rural-urban gap	100	100	100	100	100

Note: Positive values indicate an urban advantage, negative indicate a rural advantage.
Source: Calculated by the author using data from the 1991 National Longitudinal Survey of Youth.

attenders are less likely to complete a full four years.

The analysis of conditional probabilities shows that neither high school nor college attrition rates are rural students' main obstacle to a college degree. Rather, rural high school graduates are less likely than urban to pursue further schooling. Since high school achievement scores are similar in the two populations, it seems that success in rural schools is less likely to be a springboard to a college career. For rural individuals, this fact unfortunately mitigates the relatively strong rural showing in school quality and achievement. Rural workforce quality, however, doesn't necessarily suffer from lower college attendance rates but would depend on whether high achievers who do not proceed to college are more likely than low achievers to leave the local area.

EXPLAINING THE COLLEGE ATTENDANCE GAP

Monetary Factors

Since the sticking point appears primarily to be college attendance, it seems reasonable to ask why rural youth are less likely to attend college. In an age when information and geographic mobility are less costly than ever before, one could assume that rural youth see the financial, social, and personal advantages of college education in much the same way as urban youth. In Chapter 3, Paasch and Swaim found that about two-thirds of rural high school seniors aspire to professional jobs and at least some college education, only a slightly smaller share than of urban seniors. Hence, differences in rural and urban attendance rates should mostly reflect differences in high school academic preparation and income. Greenberg and Teixeira (Chapter 2) demonstrate that, while rural and urban high school students score about equally well on tests of math, reading, and science ability, rural schools are less likely to offer the advanced courses that help prepare college-bound students.[3]

The large and longstanding gap between rural and urban incomes may be the most powerful constraint on college attendance. Family income has been a consistently strong predictor of attendance in regression models with national samples. During the 1980's, median rural family income averaged about 75 percent of the urban median, according to census figures. Among young people who attended college, the NLSY sample indicates that the median family income of rural students was 87 percent of urban students' family income (Table 4.4). Rural students can narrow the income gap either by attending less expensive colleges or by obtaining larger amounts of financial aid than urban students. The evidence indicates that students use both strategies. The median tuition faced by rural students in the sample is over 400 dollars (36 percent) lower than tuition for urban students, suggesting that they do select less expensive colleges. While their tuition is lower, larger shares of rural than urban students obtain loans and grants. Among those receiving financial assistance, both rural and urban loans average 2,500 dollars, and grants to rural students average only 100 dollars less than those to urban students. The greater use of these strategies among rural students suggests that their decision to attend is more sensitive to loan and grant availability, as well as to the geographic availability of affordable colleges.

TABLE 4.4. Financial resources and obligations of college attendees

Item (unit)	Rural	Urban
Median family income (dollars)	30,045	34,500
Students receiving loans (percent)	33.1	27.0
Median amount received (dollars)	2,500	2,500
Students receiving grants (percent)	48.6	37.8
Median amount received (dollars)	1,400	1,500
Median annual tuition[a] (dollars)	747	1,174

[a] Includes students who attended either 2-year or 4-year colleges. These statistics are based on tuition rates for the 1980-81 school year, about the middle of the period when most respondents would be attending college. The comparable figures for 1990-91 are 1,800 dollars for rural and 2,552 dollars for urban students.

Source: Calculated by the author using data from the 1991 National Longitudinal Survey of Youth, the Current Population Survey, and the Higher Education General Information Survey.

Nonmonetary Factors

Family income gauges the ability to pay for college. Yet the decision is shaped as much by young people's perceptions of the value of a college degree and their expectations about their adult social and work lives. Families, social peers, and the community at large all act as forces that help to create expectations and reinforce perceptions. These forces can create positive or negative images of college life, make the transition to a college environment easy or hard, and reinforce or weaken the desire to maintain socioeconomic status at or above that of the previous generation. Families' and communities' investment in their children also contributes to students' performance on college entrance exams, to their perceptions of college opportunities, and to their decisions regarding whether or when to marry and have children.

Several variables that enter the empirical model described in the next section test the association between college attendance and family and community characteristics. One dimension of the local environment relevant to rural-urban differences is geographic access to college. It seems reasonable that living in a college town, or at least within close proximity to a college, increases the likelihood that young people have some familiarity with college life. They are more likely to have participated in the social and cultural activities colleges provide. There may have been cooperation between the college and local high schools to encourage college applications. And a local college workforce helps create the community values that reinforce the desire to attend.

Rural students face clear disadvantages regarding college information and access. About half of all rural high school students live in counties with no college, compared with 11 percent of urban students (Table 4.5). Rural areas also have fewer highly educated workers to illustrate the value of attending college or high-skill jobs to reward a college degree. About 80 percent of rural (versus 21 percent of urban) students live in counties in which less than 15 percent of the resident labor force holds a bachelor's or higher degree.

TABLE 4.5. Share of students living in areas with colleges or college-educated workforce, at age 14

County characteristic	Rural	Urban
	Percent	
No college in area	49.1	10.6
One or more 2- or 4-year colleges	50.9	89.4
One or more 4-year colleges	28.9	82.0
Less than 15 percent of local workforce has a 4-year college degree or higher	79.8	21.0

Source: Calculated by the author using data from the 1991 National Longitudinal Survey of Youth.

Sorting out the Factors

Lower rural college attendance rates, then, could arise from a combination of individual, family, and local area factors. The independent effect of each on the probability that a respondent attends college given high school graduation is estimated through the use of logistic regression, and the results are reported in Table 4.6. For ease of exposition, I have chosen to report the multiplicative effect on the odds ratio for each variable on the likelihood of attending. Values of this statistic greater than 1.0 indicate that the variable is associated with an increased likelihood of attendance. Values less than 1.0 indicate a decreased likelihood.

In the first equation, individual, family, and price/income effects are con-

TABLE 4.6. Tests for rural-urban differences in college attendance, NLSY sample

Variable	Equation 1 Individual, family, and cost/income effects	Equation 2 Plus region and local characteristics
	Multiplicative effect on the odds-ratio	
Grades	1.965***	2.015***
Black	1.581***	1.507***
Male	1.078	1.080
Age at high school graduation	0.765***	0.771***
Parents' education	5.317***	5.118***
From a female-headed family	1.369**	1.326**
Got married in high school	0.986	1.007
Had child in high school	0.613**	0.615***
Nonmover	0.825***	0.822***
Family income	1.001*	1.001*
Average state tuition	0.999***	0.999**
Siblings	0.938***	0.942***
Rural residence	0.819**	0.984
Midwest	---	0.872
Northeast	---	0.992
West	---	1.131
College/dropout wage ratio	---	1.463*
Job growth, 1975-79	---	0.994*
2- or 4-year college in county	---	1.238**
Share of college educated in the workforce	---	4.100*
Number of observations	*4132*	*4127*

--- = Not applicable.
Note: ***,**,* denote statistical significance at 1, 5, and 10 percent confidence levels, respectively.
Source: Calculated by the author using data from the 1991 National Longitudinal Survey of Youth.

trolled to test possible sources of rural-urban differences. Students with higher grade point averages in early high school subjects, who graduate at younger ages, or who have college-educated parents are more likely to attend college. Students who had children in high school are less likely to attend. The price/income variables also performed as expected. Family income at the time of the initial 1978 interview is positively associated with college attendance. Another variable is the average annual tuition of senior colleges and universities in the respondent's state university system. The higher the average state tuition, the lower is the probability of attending college. Finally, I included the number of siblings as a measure of competing demands on family income, and as expected, more siblings reduces the likelihood of attending.

Other findings were unexpected. Blacks are more likely to attend college than are whites once grade point average, income, and family characteristics are controlled, as are children from female-headed households (compared with children from other households). Despite historically low returns to education faced by blacks, they may particularly value the increased occupational status that a college degree engenders. The positive association between female-headed households and college attendance isn't predicted in the literature. It is stronger than Paasch and Swaim's insignificant findings for high school dropouts (Chapter 3), although the relationship between attainment and household head status is the same in both studies. The finding raises the possibility that the negative impact of single-parenting on attainment is largely due to lower income, which is controlled in the model.

Finally, rural residence continued to strongly and negatively influence college attendance even after controlling for the power of individual family factors. Thus lower family income and slightly lower grades in school are inadequate explanations of the rural-urban attendance gap. A second equation incorporates specific locational characteristics into the explanatory framework, which one would expect to dampen the association between attendance and rurality. I included two variables that affect the respondent's perception of the value of a college education. The ratio of the average wages of college graduates in the area to high school graduates indicates the expected pecuniary return to college.[4] Greater local availability of jobs (measured here by job growth over a four-year period preceding high school completion) provides an alternative to further education and should reduce the likelihood of college attendance. Both of these variables behave as expected—higher relative college graduate wages increases attendance, while job growth reduces it.

The "social access" variables also play a role in explaining education choices. The presence of either a two- or four-year college encourages attendance, and the share of college-educated workers in the local workforce is positively associated with attending college. The social and economic environment indicated by a large college-educated population may provide supplemental benefits, especially to those students whose families provide low social capital levels. As expected, the effect of area education levels on the probability of attending college depends in large part on high school achievement and family education levels. For students with high GPA's and highly educated families, local education levels make little difference, nor does rural residence (Table 4.7). For students with average grades and non–college-educated parents, ruralness and local education levels matter—the probability of attending college for urban students is 5 points higher in high-education than in low-education areas. For rural students, the difference is 6 percentage points. Similarly, rural residence reduces the likelihood of college attendance by 4 to 5 points, depending on area education levels.

The logistic equations above assume that the various familial, social, economic, and environmental characteristics tested have similar effects on rural and urban students' college decisions. Yet the findings hint that the social and economic environment help shape students' decision calculus, and the rural and urban environments are clearly distinct. If so, then an estimate that combines both kinds of students into a single sample misspecifies the true relationship between these characteristics and the probability of going to college. I address this by estimating an equation similar to the second one, but for rural students only (Table 4.8). The rural-only model departs from the larger sample in important ways. Most variables in the rural-only model have the same expected effect, but many are no longer significant, the chief exceptions being parental education, grade point average, and childbearing. Since all respondents live in nonmetro counties, I was able to add urban proximity—adjacency to a metro area—as a measure of access. Adjacency to a metro area is positively associated with attendance; it may capture the benefits of nearby colleges and high-skill labor markets

Table 4.7. Probability of college attendance given selected characteristics

Area characteristics	College educated parents, 3.5 GPA	Non-college parents, 2.5 GPA
	Probability of attending college	
20 percent of the local workforce has a B.A. or more		
Rural	.98	.62
Urban	.98	.66
10 percent of the local workforce has a B.A. or more		
Rural	.97	.56
Urban	.98	.61

Note: Probabilities are calculated for a nonpoor white male westerner in a 2-parent household and a non-college town. Probabilities will vary slightly if a different set of characteristics is assumed.

Source: Calculated by the author using data from the 1991 National Longitudinal Survey of Youth.

TABLE 4.8. Factors affecting the likelihood of rural students attending college

Variable	Multiplicative effect on the odds-ratio
Grades	2.087***
Black	1.294
Male	0.832
Age at high school graduation	1.013
Parents' education	7.036***
From a female-headed family	1.435
Got married in high school	0.906
Had child in high school	0.322***
Family income	1.001
Siblings	0.940*
Midwest	0.829***
Northeast	0.435**
West	1.174
Adjacent to a metro area	1.579*
College/dropout wage ratio	1.247
Job growth, 1975-79	0.991
2- or 4-year college in county	1.240**
Share of college educated in the workforce	6.145**
Number of observations	*1007*

Note: ***,**,* denote statistical significance at 1, 5, and 10 percent confidence levels, respectively.
Source: Calculated by the author using data from the National Longitudinal Survey of Youth.

(independent of conditions in the immediate area).

Of the locational characteristics, both presence of a local college and labor force education levels significantly influence attendance within rural areas, as is the case nationally. These findings suggest that the geographic break between local environments that do and do not support and encourage college attendance does not correspond closely to official metro-nonmetro boundaries. Rather, the divide separates places characterized by traditionally rural socioeconomic milieus from college towns and regional trade and service centers.

Regional differences also appear among rural students, in contrast with negligible region effects for the combined sample. These last results, however, should be interpreted with caution. Rural students in all other regions of the country are shown to be more likely to attend college than students in the Northeast, a finding that is difficult to corroborate with other research.[5]

SIMILARITIES IN RURAL AND URBAN COLLEGE CAREERS

Rural-urban differences in income, academic preparation, and access suggest that the type and location of colleges chosen will also differ. Unsurprisingly, since most students attend schools within 50 miles of home, urban students are much more likely to attend colleges in urban locations than are rural students (Table 4.9). Although only 20 percent of all colleges are located in rural areas, 53 percent of rural students attend rural colleges, pointing to the strong hold of "home," or at least of familiarity.

Rural students are also significantly more likely to attend public colleges. There are probably several reasons why this is so. First, public colleges in rural areas are more numerous and have larger enrollments than private colleges, both in absolute terms and relative to the public/private ratio in urban areas. Second, rural students are less able to afford the higher tuition that private colleges typically charge. Finally, public colleges are less likely to require advanced high school course work, which is often lacking in rural schools.

It should come as no surprise, then, that rural students are only half as likely as urban students to attend or graduate from more competitive schools. Of the 335 schools classified as "most," "highly," or "very" competitive in the 1990 edition of Barron's *Profiles of American Colleges*, only 61 are located in rural counties. Combined with lower access to advanced preparatory courses and lower family income, the physical distance from more competitive schools creates social distance as well.

TABLE **4.9.** College characteristics and selected fields of study by residence

	Attendees		Graduates[a]	
Item	Rural	Urban	Rural	Urban
	Percent			
Type of college				
Urban	46.7	88.4	54.1	85.6
Public	82.3	74.2	81.8	60.5
In-state	83.0	79.5	81.7	70.7
More competitive[b]	7.1	15.0	14.9	33.6

[a]Bachelor's degree or higher.
[b]Includes "most," "highly," and "very" competitive schools defined in Barron's *Profile of American Colleges,* 1990.
   Source: Calculated by the author using data from the 1991 National Longitudinal Survey of Youth.

Migration and Local Human Capital Change

College attendance was a primary motivation of rural young people's outmigration during the 1980's, and the loss was not fully compensated by in-migration of urban young people (Table 4.10). Rural counties experienced a net loss of 16 percent of their young population. About 35 percent of rural young people left their counties for urban areas and did not return by age 25, while a number of urban young people, equivalent to 19 percent of rural young people, moved in. About 15 percent of rural young people moved between rural counties, which had no effect on the overall rural loss of young people, but undoubtedly left some rural counties with fewer young people. Movement varies widely by educational attainment. The overall rural net loss ranged from 11 percent of high school dropouts and graduates, to 15 percent of nongraduating college attenders, to 30 percent of graduates with four or more years of college.

Migration differences by education clearly change the educational composition of the rural population. Dropouts and high school graduates comprise a much larger share of young people who stayed in rural areas than of those lost to urban areas. At the other end of the educational spectrum, four-year college graduates are only 10 percent of stayers but 35 percent of those lost to urban areas. The outmigration of young people from rural areas, then, significantly reduces overall human capital levels.

Most college attenders, about 75 percent, do move to a different county to attend school. Retaining graduates who have stayed at home and recapturing those that have left present two separate problems for local areas. Graduates away

TABLE **4.10.** Rural in- and outmigration rates by education

	Total	Dropout	High school graduate	College attendee	College graduate	Bachelor's or higher degree[a]
			Percent			
Out to urban areas	35	29	26	35	53	58
In from urban areas	19	18	15	20	26	28
Within rural areas	15	16	13	15	15	16
Net change	-16	-11	-11	-15	-27	-30
Share of total loss	NA	10	25	22	43	35
Share of stayers	NA	17	45	22	16	10

NA = Not applicable.

[a] Subset of all college graduates who include those obtaining 2-year, associates degrees.

Source: Calculated by the author using data from the 1991 National Longitudinal Survey of Youth.

from home experience more intervening opportunities and may have weaker ties to home. Graduates who attend local colleges may do so because of stronger attachments to the local area, as well as to minimize housing and/or food expenses. Hence, they may be more willing to stay after graduation.

About 25 percent of rural students stay in their home county to attend college, and 16 percent are still there by age 25 (Table 4.11). Of the 75 percent who left to go to college, about a third returned home by age 25. As a result, the rural counties kept or regained 40 percent of their native college attenders. If the definition of "home" is expanded to the local commuting zone rather than the county, the proportion who stay or return increases to 49 percent. Earlier work using 1990 Census data shows that return migration continues beyond age 25 (Gibbs and Cromartie 1994). Rural counties experienced negligible net losses of 30- to 34-year-old college graduates between 1985 and 1990.

In summary, these numbers tell yet another version of the rural brain drain story. Yet they also indicate that migration undertaken by rural students to attend college is not necessarily detrimental to the home area. True, young people often must move to attend the college of their choice, a process that weakens the links between person and home place and may ultimately separate people with newly acquired human capital from their origins. However, rural counties could benefit from losing a large percentage of their young people to outside colleges if social ties and local economic opportunities are strong enough to bring the college educated and their skills back after graduation.

TABLE 4.11. Patterns of college and post-college mobility for rural attendees

County			Commuting zone		
College		Age 25	College		Age 25
		Percent			
Home	25	Home 16	Home	40	Home 29
		Away 9			Away 11
Away	75	Home 24	Away	60	Home 20
		Away 51			Away 40
Returns/stayers		40			49
Leavers		60			51

Note: Attendees include those who did not complete college degree.
Source: Calculated by the author using data from the National Longitudinal Survey of Youth.

Causes and Consequences of Return Migration

For rural places, the return rate of college graduates is a critical indicator of the ultimate consequences of the college-bound brain drain. Places that send off large number of attenders but recapture them four or more years later clearly benefit from the migration cycle and may wish to encourage it. Overall, return migrants make up about 31 percent of the pool of college graduates in rural areas, less than in-migrants from other counties (49 percent), but more than stayers who attended locally (20 percent). Return migrants are a particularly useful group for studying area attributes that attract college graduates. Like college-educated stayers, most leavers have attachments to home, whether in the form of ties to family and friends, assets such as "the old homestead," or past employers. But like non-natives, they possess information about economic opportunities in other areas, at least the one in which they went to school, and may have formed attachments to other places, particularly through marriage.

Are the factors associated with rural return primarily personal (e.g., familial attachments), or is return governed by the strict law of wage rates and job availability? Again, I control both sets of factors simultaneously with logistic regression to determine whether either set of factors is primarily responsible for lower rural than urban return rates and whether specific factors in the return decision vary for rural- and urban-raised graduates (Table 4.12). Because of survey limitations, the estimated models cannot capture some important effects, such as past employment, friendship networks, and detailed labor market characteristics.

The first model tests only the effects of rural residence and attachments on the probability of returning to the home county by age 25. Attachments are measured by whether the respondent is female, whether the origin family was poor, whether the origin family was headed by a single woman, whether the respondent has siblings, whether the respondent had moved to his or her home after age six, and whether the respondent was married or had a child during his or her college career. Women are more likely to be cast in caretaking roles, and poor or single parents are more likely to require their children's assistance, and these characteristics should be associated with a greater likelihood of returning. Siblings, however, tend to shoulder family responsibilities and should depress return rates. Marriage and having children while away from home have potentially ambiguous effects. They signal the graduate's intention to "settle down" (and home may be viewed more positively in that context). However, they also introduce a spouse's set of attachments into the equation. Respondents who moved during their school-age years may have attachments to multiple "homes" or to no home in particular.

As it turns out, the negative effect of rural residence on returning home is independent of attachment measures. Being female, having a mother alone, marrying or having a child during one's college tenure, and having lived in one place from early childhood all increase the likelihood of returning. Having other siblings, as expected, reduces that likelihood. When distance from home (which

TABLE 4.12. Factors associated with post-college return migration

Variable	Personal /family characteristics	Plus home county characteristics	Rural graduates	Urban graduates
	multiplicative effect on odds-ratios			
Female	1.388***	1.419***	2.078**	1.277*
Family income	1.000	1.000	1.303	0.693
Female head	1.745***	2.196***	3.112**	2.171***
Marriage/child	1.713*	2.216**	3.161**	1.568
Siblings	0.483**	0.644	0.751	0.564
Moved after 6	0.497***	0.472***	0.290***	0.504***
Rural residence	0.464***	0.899	NA	NA
Distance	NA	0.731***	0.607**	0.712***
Home earnings	NA	1.104***	1.087	1.105***
Home job growth	NA	1.019***	1.018	1.020***
Home in Midwest	NA	1.081	1.240	1.068
Home in Northeast	NA	1.043	0.810	1.050
Home in West	NA	0.612**	0.071	0.640

NA = Not applicable.

Note: ***,**,* denote statistical significance at 1, 5, and 10 percent confidence levels, respectively.

Source: Calculated by the author using data from the 1991 National Longitudinal Survey of Youth.

captures both attachment and intervening opportunities) and labor market characteristics are added, in the second column, the significance of rural residence disappears. High earnings and rapid job growth in the home county appear to be strong draws for native graduates. Distance between home and college acts as a significant barrier to return. The effects of home region are unimpressive except for western home counties. Since distance is controlled (an otherwise likely source of western uniqueness), the significant and negative effect of growing up in the West confirms other studies that have found unusually high levels of population "turnover" in the West. The attachment variables continue to be positively associated with returning , except for the existence of siblings.

When rural and urban returnees are analyzed separately, the signs of the coefficients in the two estimations agree, but the sets of significant variables differ. Attachment variables appear to play a larger role for rural graduates. The positive effects of being female and of getting married or having a child on returning are much stronger for rural-raised graduates, perhaps reflecting rural-urban differences in attitudes toward the role of extended families or the intervening effects of spouses. For rural graduates alone, job growth and wage levels are insignificant predictors of return; quite the contrary is true for urban graduates.

While home ties and intervening life choices appear to predict rural college graduates' residential decision, one should be careful not to underestimate the importance of the labor market based on this analysis alone. The statistical insignificance of these variables may be deceptive, since the smaller rural sample size makes significance at a given level more difficult to attain. Similar odds-ratios in the rural and urban models, for example, point to small sample size rather than to weak labor market effects.

Another way to gauge the pull of wages and employment on rural-raised graduates is to compare their outcomes with their urban counterparts'. If we ignore postcollege residence, urban graduates have higher employment rates and higher earnings and are slightly more like to work in higher-status occupations than are rural graduates (Table 4.13). When broken down by precollege and postcollege residence, labor market outcomes differ substantially. Rural graduates who live in urban areas after college are more likely to be employed and work in managerial, administrative, or professional occupations than are (1) those who stayed in or returned to rural areas or (2) urban graduates in either rural or urban areas. However, the average earnings of rural graduates in urban areas are lower than the earnings of urban graduates who remain in or return to urban areas. Rural students who stayed in or returned to rural areas have the lowest employment rates and are much less likely to be found in white-collar occupations. The prospects faced by college graduates in rural areas undoubtedly increase the difficulty rural employers have recruiting managerial and professional staff (see Chapter 7).

In general, postcollege residence appears to be a critical predictor of labor market success, suggesting that rural graduates largely overcome the disadvantages of rural origins. The return migration models, however, show that personal factors constrain market outcomes. The pull of family ties, for example, may induce rural graduates to accept lower returns on their education, in effect lowering the economic value of their college degrees.

CONCLUSION

Lower college attendance is the single most important component of lower rural college completion rates. Rural students, on average, are less likely to have the individual and family traits associated with attendance. Thus rural-urban differences in completion rates largely reflect the geographic distribution of these traits. Yet environmental forces also operate on the individual's aspirations. Local education levels and the presence of a local college are associated with an individual's decision to attend. A more highly educated population may foster a better education system and create a social environment that supports scholastic achievement and an economic environment that monetarily rewards it.

Rural college graduates are more likely to attend rural and public colleges and universities and are only half as likely to finish at selective institutions. While these choices have possible career repercussions, postcollege plans appear to play a larger role in the economic well-being of rural graduates. Rural graduates who

TABLE 4.13. Employment characteristics of 25-year-old college graduates

Characteristics at age 25	Location at 14		Location at 14/location at 25			
	Rural	Urban	Rural/ rural	Rural/ urban	Urban/ rural	Urban/ urban
			1991 dollars			
Median earnings	25,050	27,240	24,525	25,585	21,615	27,800
			Percent			
Employment status						
Employed	81.7	84.6	75.0	87.8	78.7	85.0
In school	6.4	6.4	6.5	6.2	8.4	6.3
Other	12.9	9.0	18.5	6.0	13.9	8.7
Occupation						
Managerial/administrative	9.3	11.6	4.4	13.2	11.0	11.7
Professional	31.7	32.0	26.5	36.0	34.4	31.7
Technical	4.8	7.0	5.4	4.3	8.2	6.9
Other	54.2	49.4	63.8	46.6	46.4	49.7

Source: Calculated by the author using data from the 1991 National Longitudinal Survey of Youth.

leave the countryside fare quite well compared with urban graduates in term of employment and occupational status. Furthermore, whatever their college choice, graduates who live in rural areas after college, regardless of precollege residence, fare worse financially than urban dwellers.

These findings help explain why rural counties in the early 1990's recaptured only 70 percent of the equivalent number of their college-bound youth by age 25, reinforcing the cycle of low education levels and low college attendance rates in many rural areas. Still, over half of the rural college-educated population at this age are natives. Coming from rural areas, natives are more likely to attend rural schools and hence to stay in the local area after college. Moreover, the pull of home acts as a counterweight to the tug of better urban job prospects. The "home-grown" supply of highly educated labor, then, forms an essential part of the rural skills mix. Current trends suggest that the rural job market for college graduates has improved in the 1990's. The challenge for rural areas is to help their youth use high school achievement as a springboard to more education and to encourage further the high-skill economy that will make graduates' decision to return an easy one.

NOTES

1 Not all questions concerning college choice and family background are available in all years for all respondents. Partial samples were analyzed where appropriate.

2 For a full explanation of the decomposition method, see Das Gupta (1993).

3 The incidence of application and acceptance to college is an alternative measure of student aspirations. It would especially provide a more precise view of the links between

achievement and environment on the one hand and the motivation to further one's education on the other. This information, however, was not asked NLSY respondents.

4 The data necessary to calculate the wage ratio were unavailable at the county level. Instead, each respondent is assigned the ratio for the labor market area in which he or she resides at age 14. Labor market areas (LMA's) are county aggregates with populations of 100,000 or more defined by the strength of intercounty commuting flows. LMA's have been identified for a .45 percent microsample file from the decennial Census of Population. For more information about the construction of LMA's, see Tolbert and Sizer (1997).

5 There is one slim connection with findings in Chapter 7, where northeastern employers are found to report fewer problems with labor quality. High achievers and/or fast learners that would go to college in other places may be enticed by the region's relatively high wages to take local jobs instead.

REFERENCES

Barron's Profiles of American Colleges. 1990. Hauppauge, NY: Barron's Educational Series, Inc.

Behrman, Jere R., Pollak, Robert A., and Paul Taubman. 1989. "Family Resources, Family Size, and Access to Financing for College Education." *Journal of Political Economy* 97(2):398–419.

Cameron, Stephen V. and James Heckman. 1993. "Determinants of Young Male Schooling and Training Choices." National Bureau of Economic Research, Cambridge, MA, Working Paper No. 4327.

Das Gupta, Prithwis. 1993. *Standardization and Decomposition of Rates: A User's Manual.* U.S. Bureau of the Census, Current Population Reports, Series P23-186, U.S. Government Printing Office, Washington, DC.

Fuller, W., Manski, Charles, and David Wise. 1982. "New Evidence on Economic Determinants of Postsecondary Schooling Choices." *Journal of Human Resources* 17(4):477–98.

Gibbs, Robert M. and John B. Cromartie. 1994. "Rural Youth Outmigration: How Big Is the Problem and for Whom?" *Rural Development Perspectives* 10(1):9–16.

Hauser, Robert M. 1993. "Trends in College Entry among Whites, Blacks, and Hispanics." In *Studies of Supply and Demand in Higher Education*, edited by C.T. Clotfelter and Michael Rothschild. Chicago: University of Chicago Press, pp. 61–104.

Kane, Thomas J. and Cecilia Rouse. 1993. "Labor Market Returns to Two- and Four-Year Colleges: Is a Credit a Credit and Do Degrees Matter?" National Bureau of Economic Research, Cambridge, MA, Working Paper No. 4268.

Krein, Sheila Fitzgerald and Andrea H. Beller. 1988. "Educational Attainment of Children from Single-Parent Families: Differences by Exposure, Gender, Race." *Demography* 25(2):221–34.

Lichter, Daniel T., Gretchen T. Cornwall, and D.J. Eggebeen. 1993. "Harvesting Human Capital: Family Structure and Education among Rural Youth." *Rural Sociology* 58(1):53–75.

Tolbert, Charles M., and Molly Sizer. 1996. "U.S. Commuting Zones and Labor Market Areas: A 1990 Update." Economic Research Service Staff Paper No. AGES-9614.

CHAPTER 5

LITERACY OF THE ADULT RURAL WORKFORCE

by Elizabeth J. Greenberg, Paul L. Swaim, and Ruy Teixeira

INTRODUCTION

The importance of universal literacy to democratic institutions and the national life has long been appreciated. More recently, several major studies of workforce quality have concluded that good literacy skills have become a precondition for economic success. Perhaps the most influential of these studies was the 1992 report by the Secretary's Commission on Achieving Necessary Skills (SCANS), which emphasized the growing importance of basic academic and communication skills for workers. These conclusions, summarized in a list of "SCANS skills" (see Appendix), are playing an influential role in national efforts to improve schools, the school-to-work transition, and adjustment assistance for displaced workers.

The argument for an increased literacy threshold is easily summarized. Computers and other new technologies, as well as organizational strategies that enhance flexibility through decentralized decision making, mean that information-processing tasks are an increasingly important component of job responsibilities. In order to perform their jobs, an increasing number of workers must use symbolic information, presented in computer graphics, written manuals, and other diverse forms. Workers are also frequently required to communicate information they have collected or generated to customers, managers, or other workers. Over the span of workers' careers, continuous learning looms larger as job requirements—and often employers—more frequently change. Lifelong education and training is much more difficult for workers lacking good literacy skills.

In short, literacy is a critical threshold skill for workers in the "information age." It follows that the literacy levels of the rural workforce are an important component of rural human capital supply with far-reaching implications for the economic prospects of rural workers and their communities.

Recognition of the economic importance of rural workforce literacy need not imply that a detailed analysis of rural literacy would add much to our overall assessment of the quality of the rural workforce. Elementary and secondary schooling is the primary means for developing a literate population, and data on rural educational attainment and achievement can be analyzed directly. For example, chapters 2 and 3 of this volume indicate that high school graduation rates have improved dramatically for rural youths even as the quality of that schooling improved relative to urban areas. Although Gibbs (Chapter 4) shows that a significant rural gap persists with respect to higher education, it is not obvious that college study is required to achieve a literate workforce. Does not rural-urban parity in high school attendance and achievement imply parity in workforce literacy?

The analysis of rural workforce literacy enriches our assessment of rural human capital in two important respects. First, we need to look beyond the qualifications of future rural workers—those coming out of high school today—to assess the skills of the current adult workforce. Many of today's workers completed their schooling at a time when fewer rural than urban youths completed high school and rural achievement levels lagged. Second, literacy, in the relevant sense, is not a simple threshold, such as the ability to sign one's name or completing grade school. Rather, workforce literacy should be viewed as a continuous measure of individuals' proficiencies at performing information-processing tasks, which is related to but cannot be inferred from data on years of schooling completed or scores on academic achievement tests. The National Literacy Act of 1991 defined literacy as "an individual's ability to read, write, and speak in English and compute and solve problems at levels of proficiency necessary to function on the job and in society, to achieve one's goals, and to develop one's knowledge and potential." Fortunately, the recent release of data from an unprecedented survey—the 1992 National Adult Literacy Survey (NALS)—allowed us to bridge both of these gaps. The NALS provides a continuous and multidimensional measure of literacy skills, as applied on the job and in other nonacademic contexts, for the total adult population.

Armed with the NALS data, we investigated the literacy skills of rural adults and made rural-urban comparisons. Findings from this investigation are presented below, starting with extensive descriptive information on the literacy of the rural workforce. We follow this with some regression modeling to sort out the interrelationships between rural location and various demographic and other characteristics that affect worker literacy. We then examine the link between worker literacy and labor market outcomes, before concluding with a consideration of the policy implications of our findings.

DATA

The 1992 NALS was a collaborative project of the U.S. Department of Education and the Educational Testing Service.[1] Each of the approximately 25,000 adults interviewed was administered three tests designed to measure his or her prose, document, and quantitative literacy by simulating actual tasks likely to be encountered in life. By measuring document literacy—which includes using tables and graphs—and quantitative literacy, the NALS test instrument expands traditional conceptions of literacy to encompass the skills recently termed "numeracy." To capture the continuous progression in respondents' information-processing skills and strategies, their performances on the exams were summarized by three scaled scores, ranging from 0 to 500. Each scale is grouped into five levels, ranging from level 1, representing very low proficiencies (0 to 225), to level 5, representing very high proficiencies (376 to 500). For example, level 1 document literacy suggests an ability to locate an expiration date on a driver's license but likely inability to enter background information correctly on an application for a Social Security card. Level 5 document literacy indicates the ability, for example, to use a table depicting survey results about parental involvement in school to write a paragraph summarizing the extent to which parents and teacher agree.

The NALS also included an extensive set of background questions that recorded detailed demographic, economic, and other information on each respondent. Of crucial importance, we are also able to distinguish levels of urbanicity because we can identify the county of residence for each respondent. We use this background information to investigate the extent, causes, and implications of rural-urban differences in literacy.

DESCRIPTIVE INFORMATION ON RURAL WORKFORCE LITERACY

Analysis of the NALS data suggests that the literacy levels of rural adults vary widely but are quite low on average (Table 5.1). All three mean scores (prose, document, and quantitative) lie near the upper end of level 2 ("low"). Adults employed at the time of the survey average 10 to 13 points higher than all adults, yet approximately 40 percent of rural workers score in the very low or low ranges (levels 1-2) and appear to have limited abilities to use written and quantitative materials (Figure 5.1). These workers may be or become trapped in low-skill and low-paying jobs because they are unable to qualify—or even train—for better paying and higher-skill jobs. The corresponding amount is approximately 50 percent for all nonmetro adults, who represent the total potential rural workforce.

Do limited literacy proficiencies represent a significant economic handicap for rural workers? The implications of rural literacy scores for rural economic competitiveness can best be assessed by comparing rural and urban scores. In

TABLE 5.1. Literacy scores by rural/urban status, employment status, and age, 1992

		Distribution by literacy levels				
Item	Mean test score	Level 1 (very low) 0-225	Level 2 (low) 226-275	Level 3 (medium) 276-325	Level 4 (high) 326-375	Level 5 (very high) 376-500
	Points			*Percent*		
Total adult population						
Prose proficiency						
Urban	274.0	20.4	25.7	32.0	18.4	3.4
Rural	268.5	20.6	30.6	32.9	13.8	2.1
Document proficiency						
Urban	268.3	22.6	27.3	30.9	16.5	2.6
Rural	262.1	24.5	30.8	30.5	12.6	1.6
Quantitative proficiency						
Urban	272.2	21.9	24.9	30.3	18.4	4.5
Rural	268.4	21.5	28.2	32.6	15.0	2.6
Employed adults						
Prose proficiency						
Urban	288.6	13.4	22.9	35.6	23.3	4.8
Rural	281.7	13.4	26.8	40.6	16.2	2.9
Document proficiency						
Urban	284.3	14.2	25.4	35.2	21.5	3.7
Rural	276.6	15.9	29.3	36.2	16.6	2.0
Quantitative proficiency						
Urban	289.2	13.3	23.9	33.6	23.3	5.9
Rural	283.6	13.5	26.1	37.5	19.3	3.5
Young adults, ages 25-34						
Prose proficiency						
Urban	282.4	16.8	23.0	34.4	21.6	4.2
Rural	283.3	12.4	31.0	35.5	17.9	3.2
Document proficiency						
Urban	281.3	16.6	24.2	34.3	21.3	3.8
Rural	281.1	13.7	30.1	37.3	16.4	2.5
Quantitative proficiency						
Urban	280.9	18.0	23.0	33.2	20.4	5.4
Rural	283.7	15.0	28.0	35.9	17.1	4.0

Source: Calculated by the authors using data from the 1992 National Adult Literacy Survey.

fact, nonmetro literacy skills are somewhat lower than metro, particularly when the suburban metro area is compared with the most rural of the nonmetro areas (see the Appendix for definitions of the rural-urban continuum). This gap (Table 5.2) suggests that the most rural areas may have a workforce literacy problem when competing with urban, particularly suburban, areas. Rural-urban comparisons of the distribution across the five performance levels also indicate a signif-

FIGURE 5.1. Distribution of adults by prose literacy levels

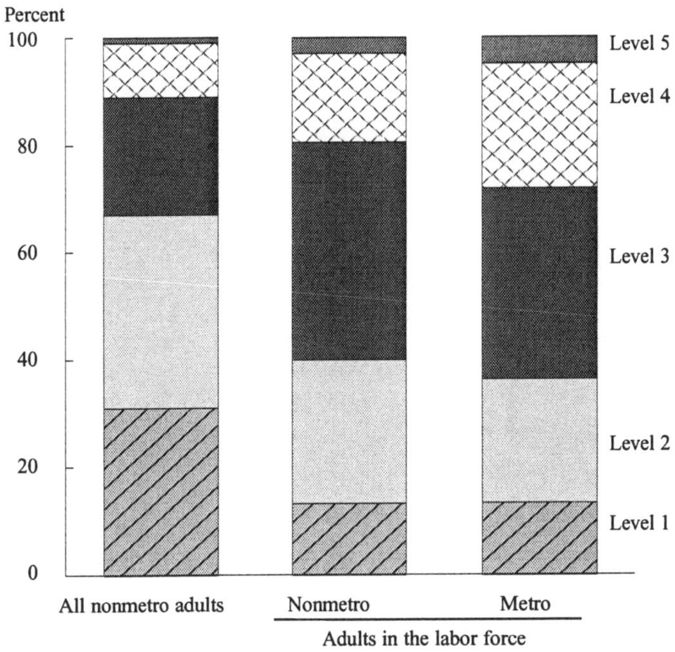

Source: Calculated by the authors using data from the 1992 National Adult Literacy Survey.

icant rural deficit in the two highest performance levels. For example, 28 percent of employed metro adults have high or very high prose literacy scores compared with 19 percent of nonmetro adult workers (Table 5.1).

MORE DETAILED LITERACY COMPARISONS

Breakdowns of the data by race, age, education, region, and other characteristics indicate that simple metro/nonmetro and rural-urban continuum averages can be quite misleading. For simplicity of exposition, when discussing these more detailed (and numerous) comparisons, we focus on mean prose scores for all adults. Unless otherwise noted, qualitatively similar conclusions hold for comparisons of document and quantitative literacy, the distribution of individuals across the five performance levels, and the employed workforce.

Perhaps of the greatest importance, the rural literacy gap essentially vanishes when attention is restricted to young adults, ages 25–34 (Table 5.3). This suggests that the rural-urban literacy gap is primarily associated with older workers who completed their schooling at a time when rural primary and secondary edu-

TABLE 5.2. Average literacy scores by rural-urban continuum, 1992[a]

Rural-urban continuum	Prose	Document	Quantitative
Metro			
Central city	272.9	267.4	271.2
Suburban	285.3	279.7	285.7
Medium	273.6	267.1	271.3
Small	275.6	270.3	273.6
Nonmetro			
Urban, adjacent	273.0	268.0	272.4
Urban, nonadjacent	275.9	268.7	277.0
Less urban or totally rural	264.7	258.3	264.3

[a]See the appendix to this chapter for an explanation of the rural-urban continuum.
Source: Calculated by authors using data from the 1992 National Adult Literacy Survey.

TABLE 5.3. Average prose scores by education, region, race, and ethnicity, 1992

Item	Urban	Rural
	Points	
Age		
25-34	282.4	283.3
35-59	279.2	284.0
60 or older	241.1	231.2
Education		
Some high school	228.8	235.4
High school graduate	267.0	275.8
Bachelor's degree	320.5	324.8
Post-graduate degree	337.0	329.2
Region		
Northeast	269.4	270.7
Midwest	280.2	277.9
South	273.5	252.2
West	274.0	290.7
Race/Ethnicity		
White	290.3	275.9
Black	241.4	213.3
Asian/Pacific Islander	241.4	NA
Other	228.9	259.9
Hispanic[a]	213.7	234.1

[a]Hispanics may be of any race and overlap with the racial categories.
NA = Mean score not reported for rural Asians due to inadequate sample size.
Source: Calculated by the authors using data from the 1992 National Adult Literacy Survey.

cation had not caught up to urban education. Consistent with this interpretation, rural literacy scores are neither consistently higher nor lower than urban scores controlling for the educational level of the respondents. These findings suggest that the rural literacy gap is on a declining course but may not fully vanish if urban youths continue to receive more college-level education.

Examination of the data by region shows that nonmetro residents in the Northeast and West actually score higher than metro residents in those regions, while those in the Midwest score approximately the same. The real metro-non-metro gap is in the South, where nonmetro residents score 21 points lower than their metro counterparts, a gap that is associated in part with the concentration of nonmetro blacks in the South. Indeed, looking at race shows some interesting variation. White nonmetro residents score 15 points below white metro residents, and black nonmetro residents score nearly 30 points below their urban counter-parts. However, Hispanic nonmetro residents score about 20 points better than metro Hispanics, many of whom are recent immigrants with limited English proficiency. (There were not enough nonmetro Asians in the NALS data set for us to accurately measure their achievement.) Looking at 25- to 34-year-olds broken down by region and race/ethnicity indicates that younger nonmetro southerners and blacks have made considerable gains over older cohorts and closed part of the gap with their urban counterparts but still exhibit below average literacy skills.

DETERMINANTS OF LITERACY AND THE RURAL LITERACY GAP

Our descriptive tabulations of the three literacy scores from the NALS indicate that rural literacy levels are modestly lower than urban—particularly suburban—literacy levels. The association between lower literacy and rural location is somewhat difficult to pin down and interpret, however, because literacy levels vary strongly across demographic groupings and regions, which are distinct from and yet correlated with urbanicity and each other. In this section, we use multivariate regression analysis to help sort out these complex relationships and shed additional light on the extent, causes, and consequences of rural deficits in literacy skills.

When the three literacy scores are regressed on urbanicity indicators alone, the associated coefficients correspond to total area differences in mean literacy. For example, in Table 5.4 the coefficient in the first row under "literacy category" indicates that mean prose scores for adults ages 20 and older were 6.2 points higher among residents of metro than of nonmetro counties.[2] Similarly, the coefficients in columns one and two indicate that residents of the largest central cities and their suburbs had mean prose scores 9.2 and 21.8 points higher than residents in the most rural counties.

Of greater interest, the regression-corrected area differences in literacy, which

TABLE 5.4. Rural-urban gaps in average adult literacy scores and scores adjusted for respondent characteristics, 1992

| Literacy category | Metro-nonmetro | Excess over 'less urban or totally rural' nonmetro area scores[a] | | | | | |
| | | Metro | | | | Nonmetro | |
		Central city	Suburb	Medium	Small	Urban, adjacent	Urban, non-adjacent
		Points					
Area differences							
Prose	6.2	9.2	21.8	9.9	11.6	9.4	11.8
Document	7.0	10.4	22.7	9.7	12.6	10.7	11.3
Quantitative	4.3	7.8	22.4	7.5	10.0	9.2	13.3
Area differences adjusted for other respondent characteristics[b]							
Prose	2.8	4.7	6.7	2.6	4.3	2.9	3.1
Document	2.6	4.1	7.1	1.9	4.1	2.7	2.3
Quantitative	1.0	3.0	5.8	-0.4	0.9	1.3	2.6

Note: Only adults 20 years of age and older were included in this analysis.
[a]The regressions contained 33 control variables for individual demographic and other characteristics.
[b]See the appendix to this chapter for an explanation of the rural-urban continuum.
Source: Calculated by the authors using data from the 1992 National Adult Literacy Survey.

are reported in the bottom panel of Table 5.4, are only about one-third as large as the total differences, although still highly statistically significant in most cases. These regression-corrected, or net, area differences are simply the estimated coefficients for the same indicator variables for urbanicity reported in the top panel of Table 5.4, once 33 additional variables potentially affecting individual literacy are added to the model. The fact that these control variables "absorb" much of the negative association of more rural residence on literacy scores confirms that the demographic, biographical, and regional compositions of rural populations tend, overall, to depress literacy levels.

What are the most important demographic and biographical characteristics that depress literacy levels in rural areas and are they amenable to policy interventions? Are there any offsetting rural advantages that raise literacy? The regression models allow us to begin to answer these questions by simulating the impact of metro-nonmetro differences in population characteristics, as measured by differences in the means of the control variables, such as dummy variables for graduating from high school or Hispanic heritage. The product of the metro-nonmetro difference in the mean value of a population characteristic with the corresponding coefficient is the regression model's estimate of how that difference in population mix either exacerbates or ameliorates the nonmetro gap in mean literacy. We calculated these compositional effects for control variables for which both the metro-nonmetro difference in data means and the associated coefficient were statistically significant at the 1 percent level. That is, we examine only the largest and most precisely estimated compositional effects.

Table 5.5 reports these simulated compositional effects for prose literacy.[3] Two characteristics of the nonmetro population significantly lower literacy levels: the higher average age and lower average education. Lower education is particularly important, with the typically lower education of nonmetro individuals and their parents significantly depressing literacy levels. Indeed, individuals' and parents' educational gaps together lower nonmetro prose literacy by 10.4 points, significantly more that the total nonmetro prose gap of 6.2 points.

The total nonmetro gap is moderated because some characteristics of the nonmetro population tend to raise literacy scores. Relatively fewer immigrants, eth-

TABLE 5.5. The contribution of differences in population characteristics to the rural-urban gap in average adult prose literacy scores, 1992

Characteristic	Contribution to Urban-rural gap
	Points
Characteristics associated with lower rural prose literacy	
Older	1.0
Less educated	
Own education	8.5
Parents' education	1.9
Characteristics associated with higher rural prose literacy	
Fewer immigrants	-2.1
Fewer Blacks	-1.0
Fewer Hispanics	-1.6
Fewer non-native English speakers	-2.4
Other (individually small) differences in characteristics	-0.9
Total compositional effect	3.4
Gap net of compositional effects	2.8
Total gap	6.2

Note: Only adults 20 years of age and older were included in this analysis. The regression upon which these results are based contained 33 control variables for demographic and other individual characteristics.

Source: Calculated by authors using data from the 1992 National Adult Literacy Survey.

nic and racial minorities, and non-native English speakers live in nonmetro areas, all groups with below-average (English-language) literacy. Despite these pluses, the net effect of all of the differences in population characteristics that we are able to control for is to depress nonmetro prose literacy by 3.4 points. The sum of this total compositional effect and the net nonmetro effect, which remains even after introducing the control variables into the model (2.8 points), yields the total nonmetro prose gap of 6.2 points.

In sum, the determinants of literacy are complex. Although literacy tends to be a little lower in rural areas, rural-urban differences in literacy are modest compared with differences in literacy across other groupings, such as education levels, race, and ethnicity. It is important for rural policy makers to take account of the low literacy of much of the rural population and of the demographic and other factors that facilitate or impede the further development of rural literacy, as revealed by these models. Our finding that the lower educational levels of older rural residents is a source of low literacy suggests—as would be expected—that improved schooling is a powerful cure for low literacy in the long run but that remedial basic skills programs for midcareer workers with inadequate literacy skills are needed to attack the core of the current rural literacy gap. It is a cause for concern that very few workers report participating in basic skills programs and that nonmetro participation is a little lower than metro (Figure 5.2). Our analysis suggests that literacy programs in urban areas should place a relatively greater emphasis on addressing the needs of non-native English speakers.

FIGURE 5.2. Share of the workforce participating in basic skills programs

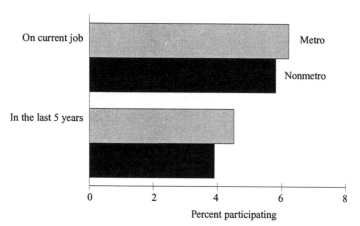

Source: Calculated by the authors using data from the January 1991 Current Population Survey for training on the current job and data from the 1992 National Adult Literacy Survey for training within the last 5 years.

LITERACY SKILLS AND THE DEMAND FOR LABOR

Now that we have some idea of the literacy differences between rural and urban areas (modest on average,especially for the young, though somewhat more substantial at the high end of the literacy skills distribution) and what accounts for these differences (mostly the demographics of rural areas), it is appropriate to turn to the demand side of the issue. How much of a demand is there for literacy skills and do rural and urban areas differ in their levels of demand for these skills?

Simple bivariate tabulations indicate that individuals with greater literacy skills are more likely to be employed and earn higher wages when employed (Figure 5.3). Do these associations indicate a large labor market payoff to bettering one's literacy skills? It is plausible that many employers value literate workers and pay a premium to recruit them. Nonetheless, caution is called for before attributing greater literacy alone to better employment outcomes because individuals scoring well on the NALS test also tend to have other characteristics that employers value, such as college degrees and similar cultural backgrounds. Multivariate analysis can help to isolate the true contribution of literacy to labor market rewards.

We estimated regression models of individual employment and earnings, which included NALS literacy scores, along with an extensive list of human capital and other control variables widely used by social scientists to predict labor

FIGURE 5.3. Average weekly earnings by prose literacy levels, 1992

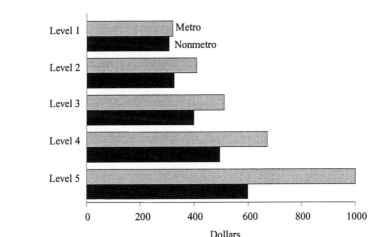

Note: Only adults 20 years of age and older, who were not enrolled in school and were employed in the week of the survey, were included in this analysis.

Source: Calculated by authors using data from the 1992 National Adult Literacy Survey.

market outcomes. Table 5.6 reports regression-corrected estimates of the impact of a 100-point increase in a literacy score on weekly and annual measures of both employment and earnings.[4] Controlling for other determinants of labor market status reduces the magnitude of the association between literacy and employment outcomes by about half, but the remaining association is highly statistically significant and of an economically important magnitude, particularly for wages. Everything else—including education—equal, a worker with level 4 prose literacy skills tends to earn 120 dollars a week (6,067 dollars a year) more than a worker with level 2 prose literacy. This finding provides strong support for the hypothesis that good literacy skills are rewarded in the labor market.

Even though the labor market payoff to literacy is high, the nonmetro gap in average literacy skills only accounts for a small share of the nonmetro gap in earnings, because nonmetro literacy levels are only a little lower than metro,

TABLE 5.6. Regression-corrected impacts of the effect of literacy scores on adult employment status and earnings, 1991-92

Literacy category	United States		Metro		Nonmetro	
	Employed week of survey	Annual weeks worked	Employed week of survey	Annual weeks worked	Employed week of survey	Annual weeks worked
	Percent	*Weeks*	*Percent*	*Weeks*	*Percent*	*Weeks*
Prose	8.2	4.6	9.5	4.9	3.9	3.3
Document	8.7	4.6	10.2	5.1	3.5	2.8
Quantitative	8.4	4.4	9.5	4.5	4.6	3.6
	Weekly Earnings	Annual Earnings	Weekly Earnings	Annual Earnings	Weekly Earnings	Annual Earnings
	Dollars					
Prose	120	6,067	133	6,821	66	3,054
Document	84	4,635	88	4,961	67	3,134
Quantitative	106	5,608	115	6,198	64	2,953

Note: Only adults 20 years of age and older were included in this analysis. For the earnings analysis, the population was further restricted to those who were not enrolled in school and were employed in either the week of the survey (columns 1, 3, and 5) or the previous calendar year (columns 2, 4, and 6). Weekly values refer to 1992 and annual values to 1991. The values reported in the table are the predicted effects of a 100 point increase in NALS literacy scores on employment and earnings obtained from regression models. In addition to literacy scores, the regressions contained 24 control variables. The models estimated for the total United States also included a control variable for urban residence.

Source: Calculated by authors using data from the 1992 National Adult Literacy Survey.

while nonmetro earnings are substantially lower than metro. For example, approximately 9 of the 128 dollar nonmetro gap in average weekly earnings in 1992 can be attributed to the 7.3-point gap in prose literacy (the 7.3-point prose gap for employed adults age 20 and over is a little higher than the 6.2-point gap for all adults.)

As to the issue of relative demand for labor across rural and urban areas, Table 5.6 also indicates that the labor market rewards for literacy are substantially lower in nonmetro labor markets than in metro labor markets. For example, a 100-point increase in prose literacy is associated with a 133 dollar increase in weekly earnings for metro workers but only a 66 dollar increase for nonmetro workers. Similarly, the probability of employment rises less strongly with literacy for nonmetro workers. Both of these patterns suggest that the demand for workers with good literacy skills is considerably lower in nonmetro labor markets than in their more urbanized counterparts.[5] Relatively low labor market rewards for literacy, in turn, probably tend to depress rural literacy because individuals have less incentive to develop these skills, while those who have high literacy tend to gravitate to urban jobs.

CONCLUSION

The results from our analysis of the NALS data can now be summarized. On the supply side, we find that there is a modest gap between the skills of the rural and urban adult workforces as a whole, which is largely attributable to older workers who grew up at a time when rural education lagged urban. The rural-urban literacy gap is much smaller for young workers, however, suggesting that, over time, the gap in average literacy skills will tend to be erased (though it is possible that the gap at the high end of the literacy distribution may remain). The very low rate of participation of adult workers in basic skills programs is thus a cause for concern because it is precisely such programs that have the potential to reach the individuals with the greatest literacy deficits.

The more general literacy problem for rural workers lies on the demand side: there are still relatively few high-skill, high-wage jobs available to reward rural workers for the skills they currently have. However, research presented in chapters 7 and 8 indicates that this situation may be changing, at least among the minority of firms that are "high adopters" of new technologies. These firms offer higher wages but also demand "new" skills (problem-solving, inter-personal/teamwork, both computer and noncomputer technical) that go beyond the standard definition of literacy. Thus, public policy, while always seeking to improve the conventional literacy levels of rural workers, should also focus on ways of encouraging a greater supply of high-paying jobs and meeting the unconventional skill demands that are likely to go with such jobs. Otherwise, efforts to improve literacy and numeracy will not achieve their full potential payoff.

Appendix

SCANS Skills

The Secretary's Commission on Achieving Necessary Skills (SCANS) identified eight areas of workplace know-how that workers need for solid job performance. Those skills are grouped into five competencies and three foundational skills (U.S. Department of Labor 1992).

Workplace Competencies

Effective workers can productively use:

- Resources—They know how to allocate time, money, materials, space, and staff.
- Interpersonal skills—They can work on teams, teach others, serve customers, lead, negotiate, and work well with people from culturally diverse backgrounds.
- Information—They can acquire and evaluate data, organize and maintain files, interpret and communicate, and use computers to process information.
- Systems—They understand social, organizational, and technological systems, can monitor and correct performance, and can design or improve systems.
- Technology—They can select equipment and tools, apply technology to specific tasks, and maintain and troubleshoot equipment.

Foundation Skills

Competent workers in the high-performance workplace need:

- Basic skills—reading, writing, arithmetic and mathematics, speaking, and listening.
- Thinking skills—the ability to learn, to reason, to think creatively, to make decisions, and to solve problems.
- Personal qualities—individual responsibility, self-esteem and self-management, sociability, and integrity.

RURAL-URBAN CONTINUUM ("BEALE") CODES

In some of the analyses in this chapter we use the Economic Research Service's Rural-Urban Continuum ("Beale") Codes, which provide a more detailed categorization of urbanization than the standard metro-nonmetro distinction (see Butler and Beale 1994). The four subcategories of metro counties are central counties of metro areas of 1 million population or more ("central city"); fringe counties of metro areas of 1 million population or more ("suburb"); counties in metro areas of 250,000 to 1 million population ("medium"); and counties in metro areas of fewer than 250,000 population ("small"). Due to insufficient sample sizes, we grouped the six nonmetro continuum codes into three subcategories: urban population of 20,000 or more, adjacent to a metro area ("urban, adjacent"); urban population of 20,000 or more, not adjacent to a metro area ("urban, nonadjacent"); and all other counties ("less urban or totally rural").

NOTES

1 For a fuller discussion of the NALS survey design and literacy measures, see U.S. Department of Education (1993).

2 In order to focus on issues related to the adult workforce, we drop teenagers from our sample when conducting our regression analysis.

3 Qualitatively similar conclusions hold for document and quantitative literacy.

4 A 100-point rise in a NALS score corresponds to a two-level increase, for example from level 2 ("low") to level 4 ("high"), and corresponds to approximately 1.5 standard deviations.

5 Supporting this interpretation of weak skill demand, we also found that, using measures of job skill requirements from the Dictionary of Occupations Titles (DOT), the skill levels of jobs held by rural workers at a given literacy level tended to be substantially lower than the skill levels of jobs held by corresponding urban workers. In addition, we found that overqualification, where the skills of the worker appeared to exceed the skills of the job, was more common in rural areas.

REFERENCES

Butler, Margaret A. and Calvin L. Beale. 1994. *Rural-Urban Continuum Codes for Metro and Nonmetro Counties, 1993*, USDA-ERS-RED, Washington, DC, September.

U.S. Department of Education. National Center for Education Statistics. 1993. *Adult Literacy in America*, Government Printing Office, Washington, DC, September.

U.S. Department of Labor. Secretary's Commission on Achieving Necessary Skills. 1992. *Learning a Living: A Blueprint for High Performance*, U.S. Government Printing Office, Washington, DC, April.

CHAPTER 6

JOB TRAINING FOR RURAL WORKERS

by Paul L. Swaim

INTRODUCTION

Intense global economic competition, rapid changes in technology, and the dissemination of "high-performance" work practices all suggest that workers with advanced skills have the best chances of enjoying high wages and job security. Historically, the rural workforce has been less educated than its urban counterpart, and rural workers have been especially hard hit by the wave of economic restructuring that first became evident during the 1980's. This coincidence suggests that many rural workers may not have enough of the right skills to compete for good jobs. By a similar logic, inadequate workforce skills may cloud the economic development prospects of many rural areas, even as the rural areas with the most highly skilled workforce enjoy an important competitive advantage.[1]

A comprehensive assessment of rural workforce skills cannot be limited to traditional schooling because job skills encompass much more than the academic skills emphasized in school. A bachelor's or professional degree is the key qualification for entry-level jobs in professional, technical, and managerial occupations. Even in these education-intensive occupations, workers typically require considerable in-service training and on-the-job experience to hone their job skills and become fully productive. For the rest of the workforce, apprenticeships and other forms of company-based training may play an even greater role in the development of job skills. Although on-the-job learning has always been an important part of the workforce training system, the importance of postschool vocational training may be increasing. Influential accounts of the emerging sources of competitive advantage in manufacturing and other sectors have emphasized the need to reorganize businesses as sites of continuous learning. Career-long employee training is seen as a key component of these high-performance competitive strategies.

In this chapter, I use data from the job-training supplements to the January 1983 and 1991 Current Population Surveys (CPS) to analyze the vocational skills of rural workers as well as their participation in postschool job training. The Bureau of the Census interviews a nationally representative sample of approximately 60,000 households each month for the CPS, which is the primary source of labor force information for the United States. In January 1983 and 1991, the standard CPS questionnaire was augmented by a series of questions concerning job skill qualifications and skill-improvement training on currently held jobs. I use this information to assess rural training patterns from the perspective of both rural workers and rural firms. From the perspective of rural workers, I examine how the access to vocational training differs, both among rural workers and between rural and urban workers. From the perspective of rural firms, I examine the extent to which these firms are pursuing competitive strategies that emphasize recruiting or training a highly skilled workforce. Barriers confronting rural firms and communities, as suppliers of job training, are also discussed.

This chapter's analysis of CPS data on job training is highly complementary to Teixeira and McGranahan's analysis of data from the 1996 Rural Manufacturing Survey (RMS) in Chapter 7. The CPS data have the advantages of covering all sectors of the economy and providing a longer historical perspective. The relationship between the training and skill qualifications of individual workers and their earnings can also be studied using these data. The data from the RMS provide a more up-to-date picture of firms' training practices and needs. Being based on interviews with managers, these data also provide much better information about how rural workforce skills and training fit into the competitive strategies that firms are pursuing. Despite these differences, both chapters reach similar conclusions, confirming the importance of specific job skills acquired after formal schooling has ended and suggesting that poor access to training providers is a significant problem for some rural firms. However, whereas this chapter documents the emergence of a significant rural training gap between 1983 and 1991, the analysis in Chapter 7 suggests that this training gap may have stopped growing, or even begun to close a little, in more recent years.

THEORIES OF JOB TRAINING

The recruitment, promotion, and pay policies of firms attest to the importance of job skills learned after the completion of formal schooling. Workers' earnings typically rise quite dramatically during their careers, suggesting that they are acquiring and refining skills employers value. For example, firms tend to recruit

or promote experienced workers with good references to fill the most demanding and best paying jobs. Economists have formalized the relationships between
investments in learning new skills—through both traditional schooling and
postschool job training—and the resulting increases in productivity and earnings
under the rubric of human capital theory (Becker 1984). Numerous empirical
studies have been conducted that indicate that human capital investments are a
principal source of productivity gains and long-run economic growth. These
studies also indicate that the productivity gains from human capital acquired
through on-the-job learning are about as large as those from formal schooling.
Career-long learning makes an important contribution to rising living standards,
both for individual workers and for the nation as a whole.

Some economic analysts believe that the economy is restructuring in ways that
increase the importance of job training. Several recent studies concluded that
extensive training of the incumbent workforce has become imperative for firms
to compete successfully in international markets on a basis other than low wages
(Dertouzos, Lester, and Solow 1989; U.S. Congress 1990; Commission on the
Skills of the American Workforce 1990). The high-skill, high-wage competitivity strategies heralded by these studies were distilled from case studies of firms
that have achieved impressive capacities for continuous innovation, quality control, and responsiveness to individual customers' needs. More recently, a nationally representative survey of employers has provided much stronger evidence of
a general productivity payoff to these new workplace practices (Black and Lynch
1996).

Computer, communication, and other advanced technologies are often necessary to achieve flexible, high-quality production. Major changes in organizational structure and business practices are also typically required because the firm
must create an environment that nurtures continuous learning and decentralized
problem solving. The exact recipe for "high-performance" work organizations
varies, but participatory decision making and extensive in-house training are
almost invariably key ingredients in the mix (Frazis, Herz, and Horrigan 1995;
Ichniowski and Shaw 1995).

A prosperous, high-skill future is not guaranteed for all workers, particularly
not for all rural workers. Some analysts caution that only a small proportion of—
mostly urban—firms have embraced the high-performance model and emphasize
that wages have deteriorated for many—especially less educated—workers
(Commission on the Skills of the American Workforce 1990; Teixeira and Mishel
1992). Concern that a significant share of the workforce could remain trapped in
low-skill, low-wage jobs strengthens the case for considering public policies that
support the maximum possible diffusion of "high-road" competitive strategies,
including measures to improve public and enterprise-based training.

A second concern is that the high-performance economy may offer diminished job security. Both the upsurge of bankruptcies and plant closings during the
1980's recessions and more recent waves of corporate "downsizing" have displaced many midcareer workers. Rural workers have been displaced at a higher

rate than urban workers (Swaim 1994). Following displacement, rural workers are unemployed longer while searching for a new job and accept larger pay cuts in order to become re-employed. Enhanced job training might lower the costs of displacement in two ways. First, workers who are able to continuously update and extend their job skills prior to being laid off should have better prospects of finding comparable jobs quickly. Second, evaluation studies suggest that public training programs, such as those funded under the Job Training Partnership Act (JTPA), can be effective for displaced workers, particularly those wanting to retool their skills and make a major career shift (U.S. Department of Labor 1995, pp. 52–56).

In sum, both human capital theory and more recent theories of economic restructuring emphasize the importance of job skills learned after leaving school and suggest that a chief determinant of the economic prospects of rural areas will be their local capacities to upgrade workforce skills. Schools play a critical role as the providers of foundational skills—including the ability to learn—required by a productive workforce. Two- and four-year colleges and proprietary vocational schools also play important roles in training adult workers, as do government training programs. Nonetheless, employers typically are the lead actors in an area's training system, both as suppliers of training to their workers and in their choices about how skills are used and rewarded within their businesses. The training practices of rural firms, accordingly, provide a valuable gauge of their competitive strategies and prospects. The economic outlook for rural workers and communities is closely tied to those strategies and prospects.

A First Look at How Rural Workers Get Their Training

The CPS data for 1991 confirm that both traditional schooling and enterprise-based training are important sources of the skills used by nonmetro workers on their jobs (Figure 6.1). Schools were the most frequently cited source of the qualifying skills workers needed to obtain their jobs (27 percent of hires), but enterprise-based training was also important. Twenty-five percent of nonmetro workers reported that informal on-the-job training (OJT) was a source of hiring qualifications while 10 percent acquired qualifications through formal company training programs. Not surprisingly, enterprise-based training was even more important as a source of skill-upgrade training after being hired, although employers also made considerable use of schools to train incumbent workers.

Nonmetro workers with hiring qualifications or upgrade training are paid more than other workers, suggesting that the training activities reported in the CPS developed skills that employers value (Table 6.1, bottom panel). The labor market premium for the skills learned from training can be estimated by the coef-

FIGURE 6.1. Share of rural workers reporting training used to qualify for or upgrade skills on current job, 1991

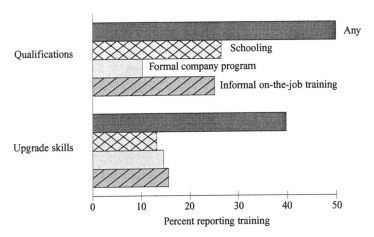

Note: Workers could report more than one type of training for job qualifying or skill upgrading, so percentages by type add to more than the total percentages receiving any training for these reasons.

Source: Calculated by the author using data from the January 1991 Current Population Survey.

ficient of a dummy variable for qualifications or training in a wage regression that also contains independent variables controlling for education and other factors influencing individual wages.[2] These regression-corrected wage premiums are substantial and highly statistically significant: 14 percent for qualifications and 10 percent for training. When separate premiums are estimated for training provided by schools, formal company programs, and OJT, formal company training programs result in the largest wage gains (18 percent). Employers apparently believe that trained workers have acquired valuable skills, especially workers who attended formal training programs managed by the firm. Viewed from a different perspective, a good way to identify firms whose competitive strategies emphasize workforce skills is to identify firms who have developed formal training programs for their workers or who aggressively recruit and reward highly skilled workers.

The training glass is also half empty. Fifty percent of nonmetro workers reported their jobs did not require any qualifying training and 60 percent that they had received no training since being hired, suggesting that many low-skill jobs remain. This interpretation is consistent with Teixeira and Mishel's study (1992), which concluded that many workers—especially rural workers—continue to be employed in low-skill occupations, some of which are among the occupations forecast to add the most jobs in coming years.

Table 6.1. Workforce training and wage premiums by residence, 1983 and 1991

Type of training	Rural		Urban	
	1983	1991	1983	1991
		Percent		
Share of workforce with[a]				
Hiring qualifications for current job				
Any	51.7	49.9	58.3	58.5
Schooling	25.5	26.5	31.7	34.1
Formal company training	8.4	10.2	10.6	13.3
Informal on-the-job training	26.2	25.1	29.1	28.1
Training on current job				
Any	36.8	39.7	36.8	43.0
Schooling	11.5	13.1	12.6	13.5
Formal company training	11.7	14.5	12.3	18.0
Informal on-the-job training	15.7	15.5	15.2	16.9
Estimated wage premium for training[b]				
Hiring qualification				
Any	16.8	13.8	20.7	21.2
Schooling	13.7	14.3	17.4	22.8
Formal company training	14.3	18.4	12.5	13.0
Informal on-the-job training	10.3	4.7	11.2	6.8
Training on current job				
Any	6.3	10.2	7.5	8.9
Schooling	3.1	1.8	6.2	6.2
Formal company training	12.5	17.7	12.3	14.9
Informal on-the-job training	2.8	6.0	1.8	0.8

[a]Workers could report more than one type of training for job qualifying or skill upgrading, so percentages by type add to more than the total percentages receiving any training for these reasons.

[b]Calculated from coefficients in semi-log regressions of individual wages on dummy variables for training. The regressions also control for education, potential labor market experience and its square, tenure with current employer and its square, and dummy variables for sex, married, a sex-married interaction, race (white, black, other), veteran, region (four), part-time job and union membership.

Source: Calculated by the author using data from the January 1983 and 1991 Current Population Surveys.

A CAUTION ABOUT THE DATA

Before analyzing rural training in greater detail, a word of caution is in order. Respondents' answers to the qualifications and training questions in the CPS interview were inevitably somewhat subjective and should not be treated as precise measures of training investments and job skills (U.S. Department of Labor 1992, pp. 1, 66–67). The CPS training supplement centered on two questions: "Did you need specific skills or training to obtain your current (last) job?" and "Since you obtained your present job, did you take any training to improve your skills?" Depending on how they interpreted these two questions, workers' answers may either under- or overstate the level of hiring qualifications and skill-upgrade training. For example, jobs may require literacy, communications, or quantitative skills that most workers view as too generic to report as a job qualification. Similarly, training that is largely an automatic result of doing a job and getting "up to speed" is also apt to go unreported by many survey respondents. My personal experience with the training programs organized by several of my employers suggests that the CPS data may also exaggerate training activities, at least in so far as they enhance productivity. Some of the training reported by workers may not have imparted useful job skills because it was poorly designed or was intended to serve other goals.

Despite this imprecision, the CPS training data provide a valuable window into firms' training strategies and workers' skills. The evidence on wage premiums strongly suggests that workers reporting qualifications or training generally are more productive than other workers, even if it is difficult to gauge precisely how much more productive. Furthermore, comparisons of training rates across groups of workers or different time periods should provide reliable indicators of differences in training because any tendency of the CPS data to over- or understate training will tend to cancel out of these differences. The rest of this chapter emphasizes such differences. The data on skill-upgrade training received by incumbent workers will also be emphasized, rather than the data on hiring qualifications, because "training" seems somewhat more concrete than "qualifications" and more closely linked to high-performance production strategies.

WHICH RURAL WORKERS GET TRAINING AND OF WHAT SORT?

The CPS data indicate that uneven access to skill-upgrade training should be of concern. Less educated workers receive much less postschool training than better educated workers and may become trapped in low-skill jobs. Just 18 percent of rural high school dropouts reported receiving training on their current job, compared with 73 percent of workers with postgraduate education (Figure 6.2). Training rates are also low for racial and ethnic minorities. Only about one in four rural blacks and Hispanics report any training on their job as compared with 41 percent of other (predominantly white) rural workers. Finally, training

FIGURE **6.2.** Share of rural workers reporting training by gender, education, race/ethnicity, and region, 1991

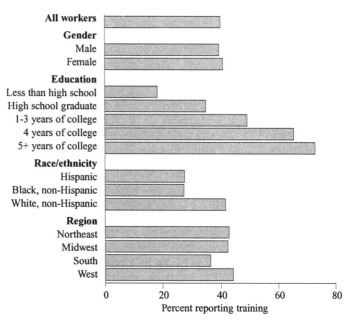

Source: Calculated by the author using data from the January 1991 Current Population Survey.

rates are lower in the rural South, where educational attainment is lowest and most nonmetro blacks and Hispanics live. These patterns suggest that enterprise-based training is least available to the least skilled rural workers, who may be in greatest need of improved vocational skills. They also suggest that the lower educational attainment of the rural workforce constitutes a barrier to postschool job training.

The training received by rural workers is quite diverse (Table 6.2). Among workers receiving training, 24 percent received training in managerial and supervisory skills, 29 percent in computer skills, and just 15 percent in reading, writing, or math skills. Fully two-thirds of the workers characterized their training as covering "other technical skills" specific to their occupation. The mix of skills targeted by training provides a useful reminder of the diversity and specificity of much job training, and of the limited overlap between postschool job training and academic schooling.

Firms also provide training in a variety of formats, with informal OJT (39 percent), formal company training (37 percent), and schools (33 percent) all playing important roles. Public job-training programs, such as those funded under the Job Training Partnership Act (JTPA), only account for a small share of the training received by incumbent workers.[3] The larger public role takes the

TABLE 6.2. Types and sources of skill-improvement training, 1991

Training type/provider	Rural	Urban
	Percent of all workers reporting training	
Type of training		
Managerial	23.7	27.9
Computer	29.3	34.7
Academic[a]	14.6	14.5
Other technical	66.4	66.9
Training provider		
School	33.3	32.0
Formal company program	37.1	42.5
Informal on-the-job	39.4	39.7
Other	14.8	15.0
If school		
High school vocational program	4.0	4.4
Private vocational school	13.3	9.7
Two-year college	41.5	41.0
Four-year college	46.8	50.5
JTPA[b]	3.7	4.9
If formal company program		
Apprenticeship	4.2	4.1
JTPA[b]	5.1	4.5

Note: Workers could report more than one type of training or more than one training provider, so percentages may add to more than 100 percent of workers reporting training.

[a]Academic programs are in reading, writing, or mathematics.

[b]JTPA are programs supported by the Federal Job Training Partnership Act.

Source: Calculated by the author using data from the January 1991 Current Population Survey.

form of two- and four-year colleges providing employees with opportunities to upgrade their skills. Public higher education appears to be an especially effective source of training for the incumbent workforce when schools tailor their offerings to the needs of specific firms or industries and offer the training as part of a more comprehensive package of industrial extension services (Rosenfeld 1992).

RURAL TRAINING UP SLIGHTLY BETWEEN 1983 AND 1991

The share of nonmetro workers receiving training on their jobs rose 3 percentage points between 1983 and 1991, from 37 to 40 percent, while the share participating in formal company training programs also rose 3 percentage points, from 12 to 15 percent (Table 6.1, top panel). Another indication that rural firms were demanding more skilled workers is that the estimated wage premium for training increased from 6 to 10 percent, despite the increase in the supply of trained workers (Table 6.1, bottom panel). Nonetheless, the modest size of these increases in training rates suggests that only a modest share of rural firms and workers had participated in a "high-performance" transformation by 1991. This conclusion is reinforced by the observation that hiring requirements do not appear to have increased, with approximately 50 percent of workers reporting qualifications in both years.[4]

Shifts in the type of training provided are also consistent with theoretical accounts of economic restructuring, but again the shifts are modest. The share of workers receiving training through formal company training programs or schools increased between 1983 and 1991, while the share reporting informal OJT fell slightly. This shift in the mix of training types is consistent with the predicted change in the composition of job skills required by the new competitive strategies and production technologies. Higher-order cognitive skills, such as how to synthesize information from a number of different sources and to engage in nonroutine problem solving, are probably best taught away from the job. By contrast, OJT is particularly effective for learning more routine or manual skills.

RURAL TRAINING LAGS URBAN

The CPS data for 1991 suggest that rural workers do not receive as much skill-upgrade training from their employers as urban workers. The rural training deficit was fairly small—40 percent of nonmetro as compared with 43 percent of metro workers had received training on their current job. It is worrisome, however, that this gap emerged between 1983 and 1991, a period in which metro training rates rose much faster than nonmetro (Figure 6.3). The rural-urban gap was also larger for formal company training programs, which probably provide a better indication of which firms are making major investments in incumbent training than does the amorphous "any training" category.[5] Although an increasing share of U.S. employers appear to believe that their long-run competitivity requires increased investment in workforce training, these employers are disproportionately located in urban areas.[6]

The types of training provided to rural workers also differ in several respects from those provided to urban workers (Table 6.2). One difference is that nonmetro workers receive less training in managerial and computer skills than metro workers, reflecting the concentration of higher-level managerial and technical activities at urban production sites.[7] This difference in the mix of training reinforces the conclusion that rural businesses lag in the introduction of high-performance work practices. Recent research has found that the effective implementation of innovative work practices, such as total quality management and teamwork, is strongly associated with increased training in communication, problem-

FIGURE 6.3. Share of workers reporting training by type of program and residence

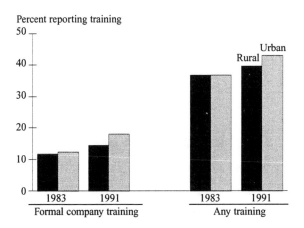

Source: Calculated by the author using data from the January 1983 and 1991 Current Population Surveys.

solving, and computer skills (Black and Lynch 1996).

Metro employment is more concentrated in the most training-intensive service-producing industries, such as finance and public administration, than nonmetro employment is. Lower nonmetro training rates are thus partly attributable to differences in broad sectoral mix. A nonmetro-metro training gap is also evident, however, within the goods-producing industrial sectors of agriculture, mining, construction, and manufacturing (Figure 6.4). Recent discussions of international competition and high-performance work practices suggest that manufacturing is a particularly interesting sector to analyze more closely. Manufacturing also employs a substantial share of the rural workforce.

Higher metro training rates in manufacturing reflect both a concentration of the most technologically complex manufacturing industries at urban sites and a division of labor within individual industries, with the most skill- and training-intensive jobs located in urban areas. When the 81 three-digit Census defined industries comprising manufacturing were divided between those using the most complex technologies and engaging in the most research and development (complex manufacturing) and those using more routine and stable technologies (routine manufacturing), complex manufacturing accounted for 51 percent of metro manufacturing employment compared with just 27 percent of nonmetro manufacturing employment in 1991 (Table 6.3). As would be expected, training rates were substantially higher for complex manufacturing. Yet only about one-third (32 percent) of the 9.2 percentage point nonmetro-metro manufacturing training gap was due to the lower share of nonmetro employment in complex manufacturing. The remaining two-thirds of the gap reflected lower nonmetro training rates within complex and routine manufacturing. Fully three-quarters of the non-

FIGURE 6.4. Share of workers reporting training by industry and residence, 1991

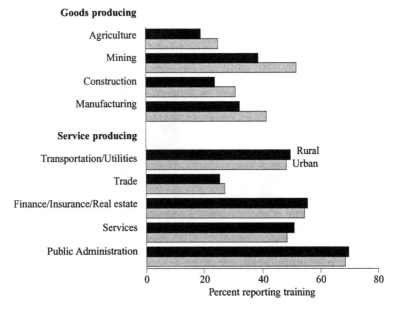

Source: Calculated by the author using data from the January 1991 Current Population Survey.

TABLE 6.3. Training in manufacturing by residence, 1991

Item	Workers receiving training on their current job:						Distribution of manufacturing jobs	
	Any training			Formal company training program				
	Rural	Urban	Gap	Rural	Urban	Gap	Rural	Urban
	-----Percent-----		Points	-----Percent-----		Points	-----Percent-----	
Type of manufacturing								
Routine	28.9	33.2	4.3	11.1	13.4	2.3	73.3	49.4
Complex	41.1	49.1	8.0	18.0	25.8	7.8	26.7	50.6
Total manufacturing								
Actual training rate	32.2	41.4	9.2	12.9	19.8	6.9	100	100
Rate using urban job distribution	35.1	41.4	6.3	14.6	19.8	5.2	NA	NA
Reduction in urban-rural gap	NA	NA	2.9	NA	NA	1.7	NA	NA

NA=not applicable.
Source: Calculated by the author using data from the January 1991 Current Population Survey.

metro-metro gap in formal company training programs was due to lower training rates within the two subsectors. Much of the spatial division of labor in which the highest-skilled work is assigned to urban sites occurs within quite narrowly defined industries.[8]

The smaller size of rural firms also helps to explain why nonmetro workers are significantly less likely than metro workers to participate in skill-upgrade training. Training rates increase with firm size, a pattern that is particularly strong for formal company training programs (Figure 6.5).[9] Many small firms probably cannot afford to establish formal training programs and must instead rely on either informal instruction from coworkers or external training providers. Regarding external providers, nonmetro firms differ from metro employers by relying more on proprietary vocational schools and less on four-year colleges (Table 6.2).[10] Rural firms are less likely to be located near four-year colleges and universities that can provide advanced training for their workforce (see Gibbs, Chapter 4), but the CPS data suggest that rural firms may have surprisingly good access to proprietary schools.

BOTH SUPPLY AND DEMAND FACTORS DEPRESS RURAL TRAINING

These CPS data suggest that rural firms train less than urban firms for both supply-side and demand-side reasons. Several supply-side conditions that dis-

FIGURE 6.5. Share of workers reporting training by size of firm, 1991

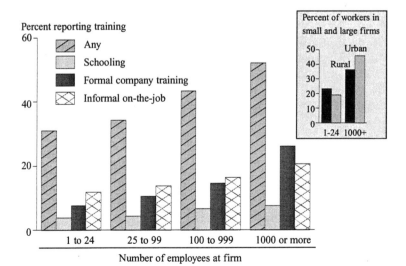

Source: Calculated by the author using data from the January 1991 Current Population Survey.

courage rural firms from training their workers have already been noted. The per unit cost for training a rural worker may be higher because rural workers are generally less educated (and less literate, see Greenberg, Swaim, and Teixeira, Chapter 5) and, hence, less easily trainable. Greater difficulty attaining scale economies in training, due to smaller firms and less access to colleges and other external providers who can pool trainees from multiple employers, also probably increases unit costs.

The example of manufacturing demonstrates that demand-side factors also depress rural training. The spatial division of labor would result in relatively low demand for skilled workers (and, hence, for training) at rural plants, even if per unit training costs were equal. The fact that the wage premium for trained workers is similar for metro and nonmetro workers suggests that demand factors are approximately as strong of a constraint on rural training as supply factors. If supply factors largely accounted for lower rural training, rural training premiums would tend to be bid above urban premiums as similar demand levels encountered more restricted supply.[11]

CONCLUSION

My analysis of the CPS data supports several general conclusions, which can now be summarized. Job skills learned after entering the workforce provide crucial qualifications for many good jobs, yet 60 percent of the rural workforce reported receiving no training since beginning their current jobs, with less educated, minority, and southern workers particularly unlikely to receive additional training. Between 1983 and 1991, the incumbent training rate for nonmetro workers rose modestly but fell behind the more rapidly rising metro training rate. The rural training gap appears to have resulted, in part, from an increased concentration of the most skilled jobs at urban production sites, which resulted in relatively low rural demand for trained workers. Supply-side factors also appear to have depressed rural training rates. The typically smaller size of rural firms, their more limited access to colleges and other external sources of vocational training, and the lower educational and literacy levels of the rural workforce probably result in higher unit training costs.

These empirical findings suggest several policy lessons. Although employer-provided training dwarfs government training programs, public assistance with meeting employers' training needs can play an important role in rural development programs targeting high-wage job growth, particularly through involving colleges and universities in these efforts. The small size and remoteness of many rural employers, as well as the typically lower education and literacy of their workforce, is a barrier to workforce training and suggests a need for adult education, job-training, and industrial extension programs to devote significant resources to outreach efforts targeted at these firms and their employees. Another concern is that current training patterns strongly favor the workers who already have the best education and job skills. Facilitating training access for less educated and minority workers accordingly represents another potential goal of government policies. It is important, however, to balance concerns for equalizing training access with the need to target training assistance where it can contribute most to modernizing rural industry.

NOTES

1 See Kusmin, Redman, and Sears (1996) for evidence that rural areas with a more educated population have tended to experience stronger economic growth. The estimated link between area workforce skills and growth would probably have been even stronger if the analysis had incorporated measures of workers' skills more comprehensive than summary measures of the years of schooling completed.

2 I follow the literature in adopting a semilog functional form for the wage equation, but I estimate separate models for the metro and nonmetro samples. In addition to the training variables, whose coefficients are presented in Table 6.1, my wage regressions included 16 demographic and human capital variables that are standard for the literature on individual earnings: education, potential labor market experience and its square, tenure with current employer and its square, and dummy variables for sex, married, a sex-married interaction, race (white, black, other), veteran, region (four), part-time job, and union membership. The estimated coefficients of these control variables conform to previous studies. See Bowers and Swaim (1994) for further details.

3 Two reasons for the limited importance of JTPA for incumbent training are the modest scale of these programs and their orientation toward serving individuals who do not have a job.

4 The CPS data actually indicate a small reduction in the share of nonmetro workers reporting hiring qualifications between 1983 and 1991.

5 The percentage point difference is only a little higher for formal company training programs, but the proportionate rural-urban gap is more than twice as large as for all training.

6 The detailed analyses of rural skill demand conducted by Teixeira and McGranahan (Chapter 7) and McGranahan and Ghelfi (Chapter 8) suggest that a growing number of rural employers adopted more skill-intensive competitive strategies during the first half of the 1990's.

7 Kusmin (1996) finds that nonmetro workers are significantly less likely to use computers at work than metro workers and that the rural gap in computerization is due, in considerable part, to the concentration of managerial and professional jobs in urban areas.

8 Indeed, anecdotal evidence suggests that a significant share of the spatial division of labor occurs within individual firms, as when research and high-level management tasks are concentrated at urban work sites and more routine production and assembly are dispersed among rural plants. Intrafirm effects can not be studied with the CPS data.

9 An important new survey of employers confirms that larger business establishments are significantly more likely to provide formal training than smaller establishments (Frazis, Herz and Horrigan 1995). Since employers' survey responses about the number of employees at a work site and whether formal training is offered are probably more reliable than workers' responses, it is reassuring that a similar relationship emerges from both sources.

10 Two-year colleges are about equally important to metro and nonmetro employers as providers of training for their incumbent workforce.

11 For rural firms, the extent to which higher rural training costs raise the cost of employing skilled workers will also be reduced if rural firms can recruit highly trained workers from urban areas. Rural areas rich in natural amenities are attracting some highly skilled entrepreneurs (Beyers and Lindahl 1996), but it seems likely that many skilled workers otherwise interested in rural job opportunities are constrained by the difficulty of finding suitable employment for their spouses. The link between migration and postschool job training is a promising topic for future research.

REFERENCES

Becker, Gary S. 1984. *Human Capital*, 2nd ed. New York: Columbia University Press.

Beyers, William B. and D.P. Lindahl. 1996. "Lone Eagles and High Fliers in Rural Producer Services." *Rural Development Perspectives* 11(3):2–10.

Black, S.E. and L.M. Lynch. 1996. *How to Compete: The Impact of Workplace Practices and Information Technology on Productivity.* U.S. Department of Labor, Washington, DC.

Bowers, Norman and Paul Swaim. 1994. "Recent Trends in Job Training." *Contemporary Economic Policy* 12(1):79–88.

Commission on the Skills of the American Workforce. 1990. *America's Choice: High Skills or Low Wages.* Rochester, NY: National Center on Education and the Economy.

Dertouzos, M.L., R.K. Lester, R.M. Solow, and the MIT Commission on Industrial Productivity. 1989. *Made in America: Regaining the Productive Edge.* Cambridge, MA: MIT Press.

Frazis, H.J., D.E. Herz, and M.W. Horrigan. 1995. "Employer-Provided Training: Results from a New Survey." *Monthly Labor Review* 118(5):3–17.

Ichniowski, C. and K. Shaw. 1995. "Old Dogs and New Tricks: Determinants of the Adoption of Productivity-Enhancing Work Practices." *Brookings Papers on Economic Activity: Microeconomics 1995*:1–65.

Kusmin, Lorin. 1996. "Computer Use by Rural Workers Is Rapidly Increasing." *Rural Development Perspectives* 11(3):11–16.

Kusmin, Lorin, John Redman, and David Sears. 1996. *Factors Associated with Rural Economic Growth: Lessons from the 1980's.* Technical Bulletin No. 1850. Economic Research Service, U.S. Department of Agriculture, Washington, DC.

Rosenfeld, Stuart. 1992. *Smart Firms in Small Towns.* Washington, DC: The Aspen Institute.

Swaim, Paul. 1994. "Adapting to Economic Change: The Case of Displaced Workers." In *Investing in People: The Human Capital Needs of Rural America*, edited by Lionel J. Beaulieu and David Mulkey. Boulder, CO: Westview Press.

Teixeira, Ruy and Lawrence Mishel. 1992. *The Myth of the Coming Labor Shortage in Rural Areas.* Economic Policy Institute, Washington, DC.

U.S. Congress. Office of Technology Assessment. 1990. *Worker Training: Competing in the New International Economy.* OTA- ITE-457. Washington, DC: Government Printing Office.

U.S. Department of Labor. Bureau of Labor Statistics. 1992. *How Workers Get Their Training: A 1991 Update.* Bulletin 2407. Washington, DC.

U.S. Department of Labor. Office of the Chief Economist. 1995. *What's Working (and What's Not): A Summary of the Economic Impacts of Employment and Training Programs.* Washington, DC.

CHAPTER 7

RURAL EMPLOYER DEMAND AND WORKER SKILLS

by Ruy Teixeira and David A. McGranahan

INTRODUCTION

C hapters 1 through 6 of this volume have primarily examined the supply side of rural education and training. Research has been presented on the effectiveness of rural teachers and school organization, on the achievement levels of rural students, on high school completion rates and college attendance in rural areas, on the literacy and numeracy skills of the rural workforce, and on training provided in rural workplaces. In the process, much has been learned about the weaknesses and the surprising strengths of the rural education and training system. And one theme that has emerged consistently from these assessments is the critical role of employer demand in determining the effectiveness of this system. That is, without greater demand for workers with high skills (the "high-skill path"), there is an intrinsic limit—a limit that may already have been reached in some instances—to the payoff rural areas can expect from education and training activities. Thus, enhanced education and training efforts in rural areas only make sense as part of an integrated development strategy that takes the central role of employer demand into account.

But, if this judgement is accurate, the abundant data presented up to this point are incomplete in an important respect: there is little direct information on employer skill demand in rural areas and whether this has been changing over time. Moreover, there is little information on which specific skills employers seek the most and have the most problems finding. How to integrate rural education and training programs with employer demand, a critical element of these programs' effectiveness, therefore remains unclear.

Fortunately, a survey recently conducted (summer 1996) by the Economic Research Service (ERS) helps fill this gap. The Rural Manufacturing Survey (RMS) provides relevant data collected directly from over 2,800 rural (non-metropolitan) manufacturing firms, about 7 percent of all rural manufacturers, as well as from over 1,000 urban (metropolitan) manufacturers.[1] Respondents were asked to provide information on locational problems of manufacturers, changing skill requirements of jobs, problems finding job applicants with different skills, training practices in the workplace, and much more.

Thus, the survey records how employers themselves view the rural workforce, regardless of the statistics on achievement, school quality, literacy, etc. In a sense, this is the critical measure of the quality of the rural labor supply. If employers can't find the workers/skills they need, rural competitiveness is compromised, and with it prospects for long-term growth in labor demand.

LOCATIONAL PROBLEMS OF RURAL MANUFACTURERS

A logical first step in this context is to look at the problems manufacturers face at their locations and to assess labor's role as a locational problem. In this way we gauge the effect of labor quality on rural competitiveness.

The quality of available labor was by far the problem most often cited by rural manufacturers about their location (Table 7.1). Three out of four of the respondents indicated that this was at least a minor problem, and nearly half of these, over a third of the rural sample, reported it to be a major problem. The problem is as likely to be cited in urban areas as in rural, a surprising result since labor skills have been held by many to be a chief reason that more manufacturers don't locate in rural areas.[2]

Following labor, taxes and environmental regulations are the most cited problems. These results are perhaps less unexpected, since they are direct government impositions. The next most important rural problem is the "attractiveness of area to managers and professionals," which was much more frequently cited by rural than by urban employers. Rural respondents also reported more problems with the quality of local schools, access to training programs, and transportation infrastructure, but these tended to be minor problems in comparison with labor quality, taxes, and environmental regulations.

Geographical Variation within Rural Areas

The quality of local labor does not appear to be quite as problematic in the Northeast, where state and local taxes are clearly the major issue (Table 7.2). More detailed analysis suggests that the perceived quality of labor problem is lowest in the more rural parts of the Northeast, most notably Appalachian

TABLE 7.1. Locational factors reported by manufacturers as problems in their establishment's ability to compete

Locational factors[b]	Any problem[a]		Major problem	
	Urban N=1044	Rural N=2787	Urban N=1044	Rural N=2787
	Percent			
Quality of available local labor	71.9	74.9	33.0	34.3
State and local tax rates	72.6	64.1	30.5	22.4
Environmental regulations	58.4	57.5	23.0	21.4
Attractiveness of area to managers and professionals	30.5	47.5	7.5	14.8
Quality of primary and secondary schools	32.0	36.6	8.3	10.2
Access to training courses	28.1	44.9	5.4	8.9
Access to airport facilities and services	15.9	44.1	1.8	8.9
Cost of facilities and land	54.1	38.4	18.4	8.2
Water and sewer systems	25.0	31.2	6.1	7.9
Local cost of labor	46.3	36.4	2.1	7.3
Interstates and major highways	15.2	26.4	3.5	6.8
Access to material suppliers	28.5	39.5	3.1	6.5
Railroad access	9.4	20.7	1.8	6.4
Access to major customers	31.3	36.9	6.1	6.4
Local roads and bridges	21.1	30.2	3.8	5.6
Access to market information	30.7	33.7	6.2	5.3
Access to equipment suppliers	22.2	34.2	2.3	5.0
Access to financial institutions	21.8	23.6	5.2	4.1
Local management-labor relations	24.3	27.0	3.4	3.7
Police and fire protection	11.4	17.2	2.1	1.6
Access to business services	12.1	19.9	1.3	1.4

[a]Major or minor problem.
[b]Ordered by proportion of rural respondents indicating factor is a major problem.
Source: ERS Rural Manufacturing Survey, 1996.

Pennsylvania. However, chronically high unemployment and higher educational levels in these areas may make labor both more reliable and more highly skilled than in other regions. Manufacturers are most likely to report a major problem with the quality of available labor in the rural Midwest, higher even more often than in the rural South.

Rural areas can also be broken down by the extent of their rurality. At one extreme are counties adjacent to metropolitan areas and with urban populations of 20,000 or more residents. At the other extreme are counties not adjacent to metropolitan areas and having no population in towns of 2,500 or more. Consistent with metro-nonmetro differences, manufacturers in the most rural counties have more problems with attracting managers and professionals and

TABLE 7.2. Locational factors reported by rural manufacturers as major problems in their establishment's ability to compete, by region

Locational factors[a]	Northeast N=304	Midwest N=1065	South N=1121	West N=297
		Percent		
Quality of available local labor	28.0	36.2	34.8	31.5
State and local tax rates	41.5	23.7	14.9	26.3
Environmental regulations	26.1	21.4	17.6	31.1
Attractiveness of area to managers and professionals	11.6	15.7	15.7	11.6
Quality of primary and secondary schools	8.2	7.6	14.1	6.7
Access to training courses	10.5	7.5	9.0	12.2
Access to airport facilities and services	7.7	8.7	9.4	8.8
Cost of facilities and land	13.7	7.1	5.6	16.5
Water and sewer systems	8.3	8.2	6.5	11.4
Local cost of labor	7.8	6.6	7.1	9.8

[a]Ordered by proportion of all rural respondents indicating factor is a major problem; top 11 factors are reported here.
Source: ERS Rural Manufacturing Survey, 1996.

with access to training courses, airports, and equipment suppliers, all issues particularly relevant to advanced technology users (Figure 7.1). Moreover, the most rural locations seem to offer relatively few advantages over the most urban nonmetro counties. The costs of labor and land and facilities are rarely mentioned as problems in remote rural counties, but they are also rarely cited as major problems in the more urbanized rural areas. The quality of available labor, on the other hand, is the most frequently cited major problem in both the most urban and most rural of the nonmetropolitan counties (as well as the counties in between). Thus, with some minor exceptions, perceived problems with the quality of available labor exhibit little geographical variation within rural areas. Perceptions of labor quality are much more closely related to firm characteristics, such as use of technology.

Locational Problems of Technology "High Adopters"

Rural manufacturers who have adopted a relatively large number of new production technologies, forms of work organization, and telecommunications generally have more highly educated workforces, pay higher wages, and have had greater employment growth in the last three years than other manufacturers. Such "high adopters" epitomize the high-skill path in rural areas and suggest its benefits. Their perceptions of problems related to location are obviously a key indicator of the feasibility of this approach in rural areas.

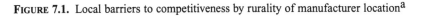

FIGURE 7.1. Local barriers to competitiveness by rurality of manufacturer location[a]

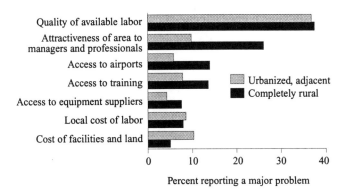

Percent reporting a major problem

[a]See text for explanation of rurality.
Source: ERS Rural Manufacturing Survey, 1996.

The RMS data show clearly that rural high adopters have more problems with human resources and access than other manufacturers. For example, compared with both rural "low adopters" and urban "high adopters," rural high adopters are somewhat more likely to report problems with the quality of available labor. Moreover, rural high adopters are nearly twice as likely to report problems with attracting managers and professionals, access to training, access to airports, and access to equipment suppliers, all critical competitive factors in these types of enterprises (Figure 7.2). For high adopters as for all manufacturers, rural areas offer advantages in labor and land costs and taxes, but there are clearly rural costs associated with the adoption of new technology. While these problems do not appear to have inhibited the rural adoption of new technology[3]—indeed, the RMS shows only a modest rural-urban technology adoption gap—they may have made these technologies less effective in rural areas.

In addition to asking about barriers to competitiveness, the survey also asked about specific problems with the adoption of new technology and forms of work organization. While problems with the availability of technical assistance and obtaining sufficient capital were not trivial for manufacturers who had adopted new technologies, human resources problems were clearly paramount. Over 40 percent of rural high adopters reported a major problem with the adequacy of labor skills, similar to the percent of urban high adopters with such a problem, but much higher than among rural low adopters. In addition, employee turnover was also reported to be a major problem by 20 percent of high-adopting rural manufacturers. However, this figure was no higher than among rural low adopters (and generally this problem was much reduced among employers paying relatively high wages).

FIGURE 7.2. Local barriers to competitiveness by technology use and location of manufacturer

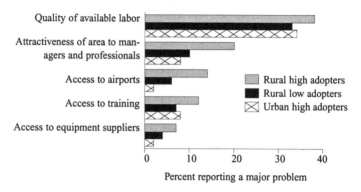

Percent reporting a major problem

Source: ERS Rural Manufacturing Survey, 1996.

IS THE RURAL WORKFORCE UNDERSKILLED?

These findings raise the issue of the content of the labor quality problems reported by rural manufacturers. Is rural manufacturing starting to enter the "new economy," thereby requiring skills of rural workers they do not currently have? And, if so, which skills? Or is some other aspect of labor quality responsible for at least some of these problems?

Changes in the Skill Requirements of Jobs

The RMS asked manufacturers whether the skill requirements of jobs for production workers had changed over the last three years. And, going beyond previous surveys,[4] the RMS asked about a number of different kinds of skill requirements: basic reading, basic math, problem-solving, interpersonal/teamwork, computer, and technical, other than computer. The results are displayed in Table 7.3.

Where changes in skill requirements were taking place, they were almost all upward. Very few rural employers—1 percent or less—reported decreases in skill requirements.

But there was significant variation in the rate of increase observed for different skill requirements. The most rapid rates of change were in computer skills and interpersonal/teamwork skills (32 percent of employers reported that these skills requirements had increased a lot in the last three years), closely followed by problem-solving skills (29 percent said skill requirements had increased a lot).

Substantially less rapid rates of change were reported for the other three skill requirements: technical skills other than computer (17 percent said needed skills

TABLE 7.3. Changes in skill requirements among rural manufacturers, 1993-96

| | Increased | | Stayed | | Rural-urban |
	a lot	a little	the same	Decreased	difference[a]
					Percentage
	----------------------*Percent*-----------------------				*point*
Computer	32	32	32	0	-7*
Interpersonal/teamwork	32	29	37	1	-2
Problem-solving	29	32	37	1	0
Non-computer technical	17	38	42	1	-1
Basic math	16	32	50	1	1
Basic reading	13	26	60	1	-1

[a]Difference between rural and urban areas in the "increased a lot" category (rural percentage minus urban percentage).
*Rural-urban difference is significant at the 95 percent level of confidence.
Note: Rows may not sum to 100 since "don't know" responses are not included in table.
Source: ERS Rural Manufacturing Survey, 1996.

increased a lot), basic math skills (16 percent), and basic reading skills (13 percent). Indeed, for the latter two skills, most rural employers reported that skill requirements had stayed the same over the last three years.

So the data suggest that skill requirements of jobs are being upgraded in rural areas but that this upgrading is strongest for computer, interpersonal, and problem-solving skills. The demand for basic academic skills, in contrast, seems relatively stable.

Problems Finding Skilled Workers

These data are intriguing and suggest that the rural manufacturing sector is beginning to participate fairly substantially in the new economy. But the critical issue here, of course, is whether this skill upgrading is creating difficulties finding workers with adequate skills. To test this, we asked a series of questions about problems finding qualified workers, both generally and in terms of specific skills. The results suggest that, while most employers encounter some problems finding qualified workers, major problems are not common and the most common problem has nothing to do with rising skill requirements per se.

Most rural employers (62 percent) do report at least some problems finding qualified applicants for production jobs. (In contrast, 42 percent report problems finding qualified applicants for professional or management jobs). When employers were asked about finding applicants with specific skills, the most common problem cited was finding applicants with "a reliable and acceptable work attitude" (Table 7.4). Many employers reported at least a minor problem in this area, and 31 percent reported a major problem.

The next most common problems were finding applicants with problem-solv-

TABLE 7.4. Rural manufacturers reporting problems finding qualified applicants for production jobs

| | Any Problem | | | Rural-urban |
	Major	Minor	No problem[a]	difference[b]
				Percentage
	--------------------*Percent*----------------------			*point*
Reliable and acceptable				
work attitude	31	25	45	3*
Problem-solving	22	29	49	1
Non-computer technical	21	25	53	-2
Computer	16	23	60	1
Interpersonal/teamwork	15	33	52	3*
Basic math	12	30	57	-2
Basic reading	5	27	68	-3*

[a]Includes those respondents who said they had no overall problems finding qualified production workers and therefore were not asked about the specific skill problems in the table.

[b]Difference between rural and urban areas in the "major problem" category (rural percentage minus urban percentage).

*Rural-urban difference is significant at the 95 percent level of confidence.

Note: Rows may not sum to 100 since "don't know" responses are not included in table.

Source: ERS Rural Manufacturing Survey, 1996 .

ing skills (22 percent reported a major problem) and technical skills other than computer (21 percent), followed by computer skills (16 percent), and interpersonal/teamwork skills (15 percent). Interestingly, rural employers were particularly likely to report no problems at all (60 percent) finding qualified applicants with computer skills, despite their report that demand for computer skills was increasing faster than demand for most other skills.

Rural employers were least likely to report major problems finding qualified production job applicants with basic math (12 percent) and basic reading (5 percent) skills. For the latter skill, in fact, over two-thirds (68 percent) said they had no problems at all in this area.

Despite the significant increases in skill requirements for rural manufacturing jobs, major problems finding qualified applicants are not common. To the extent there are major problems, they are associated most strongly with problem-solving and noncomputer technical skills. But the most commonly reported problem—a reliable and acceptable work attitude—has nothing to do with rising skill requirements as conventionally defined.

Whatever the origin of problems finding qualified production workers, about half of employers say that their problems have increased over the last three years. Two-fifths say their problems have remained the same, and just 9 percent say problems have decreased. But, while their problems finding qualified applicants may be increasing, rural employers at this point still see the overwhelming majority of production workers—74 percent on average—as being fully proficient at their jobs (though this figure was lower among manufacturers who reported major skill problems).

Skill Problems of Technology High Adopters

Earlier in this chapter, we established that high adopters of new technology experienced more locational problems, including problems with the quality of available labor, than did low adopters. Does this pattern extend to the skill problems just discussed? If so, this might indicate that, while skill problems seem quite moderate among rural manufacturers as a whole, among those leading the way into the new economy skill problems are more serious.

Analysis of the RMS data supports this conjecture. High adopters—about one-fifth of rural firms—report substantially higher rates of increase in skill requirements than low or medium adopters. For example, 53 percent of high adopters said problem-solving skill requirements had increased a lot in the last three years, compared with just 29 percent of medium adopters and 10 percent of low adopters. There are similar differences among adopter groups for the other skill requirements.

These results certainly suggest that high adopters may have more difficulty finding workers with certain skills, since skill requirements at their firms are changing so rapidly. Other RMS data confirm this. For every type of skill, with one important exception, high adopters are substantially more likely than low adopters to report major problems finding production workers with that skill (Figure 7.3). The largest disparities in reported problem areas are problem-solving skills and noncomputer technical skills where over 30 percent of high adopters report major problems, compared with just 17 and 11 percent respectively of low adopters.

FIGURE 7.3. Rural manufacturer problems finding qualified workers by technology use

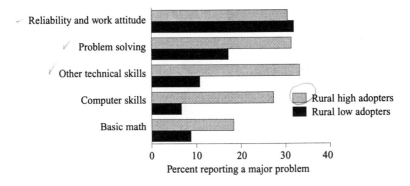

Source: ERS Rural Manufacturing Survey, 1996.

Not only are high adopters substantially more likely to encounter major skill problems, but they are particularly likely to encounter such problems in low-education counties where, presumably, skills among the adult workforce are relatively low (Figure 7.4). For example, over 40 percent of high adopters report a major problem finding workers with adequate problem-solving skills in counties where less than 75 percent of young adults (ages 25–44) have at least a high school diploma, compared with under 30 percent of high adopters in counties where more than 90 percent of young adults have a high school degree.

There is one exception to the higher problem rates of high adopters. Both high and low adopters are equally likely to report major problems finding workers with a reliable and acceptable work attitude (about 30 percent in each case). However, high adopters have greater reliability problems only where local education levels are lowest (Figure 7.5). Almost 40 percent of high-adopting manufacturers report such problems where high school graduation levels dip below 75 percent.

Thus, high adopters not only are substantially more likely to encounter problems finding workers with specific skills—especially problem-solving and non-computer technical skills—but they also have the same problems as other manufacturers finding reliable workers. And these problems are exacerbated for high adopters where local educational levels are low. All this suggests that, while skill problems may not be particularly important for most rural manufacturers, among

FIGURE 7.4. Rural problems finding production workers with problem-solving skills, by technology use and county education level

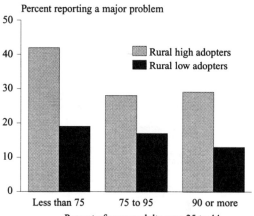

Source: ERS Rural Manufacturing Survey and the 1990 Census of Population.

FIGURE 7.5. Rural problems finding production workers with acceptable and reliable work attitudes, by technology use and county education level

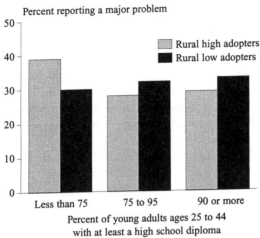

Percent reporting a major problem

Rural high adopters
Rural low adopters

Less than 75   75 to 95   90 or more

Percent of young adults ages 25 to 44
with at least a high school diploma

Source: ERS Rural Manufacturing Survey and the 1990 Census of Population.

the minority that are leading the way into the new economy, skill problems present serious obstacles to further development.

Training Practices of High Adopters

Given the skill problems experienced by high adopters, we would expect them to emphasize training. The RMS data show that, though only a minority of rural manufacturers (48 percent) currently provide formal training for their production workers, among high adopters that proportion soars to 77 percent (compared with just 40 percent among low/medium adopters).

Similarly, among the high adopters who did provide training, an overwhelming 82 percent had increased the amount of that training in the last three years, including 44 percent who said they had increased training a lot over that time period. In contrast, low/medium adopters who provided training were less likely to have increased that training in the past three years (66 percent) and included only 26 percent who said they had increased training a lot.

Interestingly, in terms of the importance assigned to the declining quality of new hires, there was little difference between high and low/medium adopters who had increased training. Only 38 and 37 percent respectively said this problem was a very important motivation for such increases. Evidently, high adopters are less motivated by a diminution in the quality of available labor than by bringing available labor in line with their own increasing skill demands.

COMPARING URBAN AND RURAL MANUFACTURERS

So far, the data suggest that labor quality problems are perhaps the chief obstacle confronting rural manufacturers, but that problems with the skills, as opposed to the reliability, of rural labor are concentrated among high adopters of new technologies and management practices—the leading edge of the new economy in rural areas.

To what extent does this situation constitute a competitive disadvantage for rural manufacturers? A partial answer can be gleaned by comparing their skill demands and problems with those of urban manufacturers. A rural disadvantage would be indicated if rural manufacturers are having a particularly difficult time compared with their urban counterparts.

Our findings, however, do not suggest such a disadvantage. As Table 7.3 shows (final column), skill requirements at rural manufacturing establishments are increasing about as fast as at urban establishments, with one exception (computer skills). Rural manufacturers appear just as willing as their urban counterparts to raise skill requirements to meet new economy production standards, an assessment supported by the fact that nearly as many rural manufacturers as urban (21 to 24 percent) are high adopters of new technology.

Even more convincing, Table 7.4 shows only very slight rural-urban differences in major problems finding applicants with specific skills. These differences top out at 3 percentage points, one of which (basic reading) is a difference that favors rural areas and another of which (reliable and acceptable work attitude) is not a skill as traditionally defined.

Combined with other data that show no rural-urban difference in the difficulty of finding qualified production workers, no difference in the perceived adequacy of production workers, and no difference in the importance attached to poorly skilled production workers as a motivation for increased training, these findings suggest that, if there is a problem with underskilled workers, it is probably a nationwide phenomenon not a rural one. Therefore, skill shortages among workers may be less a source of rural competitive disadvantage than a problem that manufacturers, regardless of location, have to address to prosper in the increasingly international marketplace.

It could be argued that the similarity in reported incidence of skill problems among rural and urban manufacturers reflects mostly an adjustment on the part of rural manufacturers to an inferior labor pool. These manufacturers may demand less of rural workers, hence their level of dissatisfaction does not exceed that of more demanding urban employers.

This line of reasoning seems implausible, however, given that the level of high-adopting manufacturers (who presumably have higher skill demands) in rural and urban areas is roughly similar. And, even more telling, the incidence of skill problems among high adopters in rural and urban areas is about the same (if anything, slightly higher in urban areas). Thus, rural manufacturers do not appear to be demanding less of rural workers, nor do they appear to be more disappointed when they make high skill demands. All this supports the interpretation that rural and urban manufacturers face similar challenges in adapting their workforces to the new economy, rather than that rural manufacturers have a competitive disadvantage relative to urban areas.

SKILLS AND LABOR QUALITY LOCATIONAL PROBLEMS

The picture of employer demand for labor in rural areas may be further clarified by examining the relationships between the two major types of data on employer demand considered thus far: (1) manufacturers' skill requirements and skill problems and (2) reported labor quality problems with manufacturers' locations.

The examination turns up some straightforward (and expected) relationships: skill requirements are rising faster at firms that report labor quality as a major locational problem, and firms that report major problems finding workers with specific skills are much more likely to report a major labor quality locational problem.

But which skill problems play a leading role in creating an overall locational problem with labor quality? Here we turned to regression analyses to compare the explanatory power of different skill problems. These regression analyses show that all skill problems, except problems finding workers with basic reading skills, are significant predictors of a major locational problem. However, easily the most powerful predictor of a labor quality problem is a major problem finding workers with a reliable and acceptable work attitude. This finding is consistent with earlier findings on the relative importance of finding reliable workers to most rural manufacturers' labor problems.

The second most powerful predictors of a general labor quality locational problem were problems finding workers with noncomputer technical skills and, interestingly, workers with basic math skills. The latter problem, as discussed earlier, is not common, but these findings say that, where it exists, it is an important influence on overall labor market problems.

The pattern just described holds up fairly well when rural firms that are low/medium adopters are looked at separately. However, when firms that are high adopters are singled out, the pattern is substantially different. While finding reliable workers continues to be the most powerful predictor, finding workers with adequate noncomputer technical skills is almost as closely associated with a major labor quality locational problem. This underscores the special problems high adopters of new technology apparently face in rural labor markets.

Skills and Regional Variation in Labor Quality Locational Problems

As noted earlier, the quality of available labor was the mostly widely cited major locational problem in every region except the Northeast. This suggests that rural employers in the Northeast either require fewer skills, draw on better equipped workers, or avoid labor market problems by some other mechanism.

The RMS data on skills confirm that rural employers in the Northeast are less likely to encounter general problems finding qualified applicants for production jobs and less likely to have problems finding applicants with specific skills, particularly workers with a reliable and acceptable work attitude.

But the data show little evidence that skill requirements of Northeast rural employers are rising less rapidly than in the rest of the country—in fact, if anything, the reverse is the case (though the difference is small). Nor do the data suggest that the educational qualifications of rural Northeast workers are much higher than in the rest of the country. Indeed, workers in the Midwest and West are quite comparable.

Where rural Northeast workers do differ is in their rates of pay: they are significantly higher than in other rural areas of the country. This may go some way toward explaining rural Northeast manufacturers' comparative lack of labor market difficulties, particularly in terms of finding reliable workers. Higher pay probably facilitates access to the best workers and helps ensure their loyalty and, therefore, reliability.

CONCLUSION

The findings from the RMS presented in this chapter considerably clarify our picture of employer demand in rural areas. In the process, they suggest some impressive strengths of the rural workforce and rural economy, strengths that are consistent with findings from other chapters in this volume. And the RMS findings also suggest some important challenges for the rural education and training system, challenges that again are consistent with analyses presented in other chapters.

In terms of strengths, the RMS findings confirm analyses (see Chapter 8) showing rural manufacturers starting to participate in a more equal way in the high-skill, new economy part of the manufacturing sector. And the RMS findings confirm that the skills of typical rural workers match up well with those of their urban counterparts (see chapters 2 and 5) and do not appear to pose a significant handicap—relative or otherwise—to most rural manufacturers. Finally, analysis of the RMS suggests that the basic cognitive (verbal and mathematical) skills of rural workers are in particularly good shape and pose few significant barriers to manufacturing employers.

On the other hand, RMS findings indicate some important challenges. For example, skill requirements are rising fairly rapidly for a set of skills—computer, interpersonal/teamwork, and problem-solving—that are not traditionally covered by the education and training system. And, among "high adopters" of new technologies and management practices, the demand for such skills is rising exceptionally rapidly and leading to fairly high incidences of reported skill problems (though no higher in rural than in urban areas). This suggests that rural participation in the new economy depends less on remedial skill training for the rural workforce than on facilitating the acquisition of cutting-edge "new skills" by these workers (see chapters 5 and 6).

Finally, the RMS data show that the most common reported skill problem is for a "skill" not usually thought of in those terms: a reliable and acceptable work attitude. This suggests that many rural manufacturers' labor problems have less to do with a skills problem as conventionally defined than with difficulties attracting the best and most reliable rural workers, given prevailing wage rates. Since reliability is relatively impervious to formal training efforts, rural areas may wish to address this workforce problem by seeking to attract employers who encourage reliability through higher wages.

NOTES

1 Technical details about the survey are provided in Gale (1997a).

2 A different reading of the term "labor quality" (reliability) might be taken as a reason for employers to be attracted to rural areas, since low-cost, reliable labor has been historically assumed to be a rural comparative advantage. On either reading, the lack of any current significant difference between rural and urban areas on this measure remains of interest.

3 See Gale (1997b).

4 See, for example, Osterman (1993) and National Center on the Educational Quality of the Workforce (1995).

REFERENCES

Gale, Fred. 1997a. *The 1996 Rural Manufacturing Survey: Technical Documentation.* Rural Manufacturing Survey Issue Brief. Washington, DC: Economic Research Service, U.S. Department of Agriculture.

_____. 1997b. *Is There a Rural-Urban Technology Gap?* Rural Manufacturing Survey Issue Brief. Washington, DC: Economic Research Service, U.S. Department of Agriculture.

National Center on the Educational Quality of the Workforce. 1995. "First Findings from the EQW National Employer Survey." EQW Catalog Number: RE01.

Osterman, Paul. 1993. "How Common is Workplace Transformation and Who Adopts It?" *Industrial and Labor Relations Review* 47, no. 2:173-88.

CHAPTER 8

CURRENT TRENDS IN THE SUPPLY AND DEMAND FOR EDUCATION IN RURAL AND URBAN AREAS

by David A. McGranahan and Linda M. Ghelfi

INTRODUCTION

What kinds of job opportunities are being created in rural areas? Do they require ever higher levels of education? Or are high-education jobs increasingly urban jobs? Anecdotal evidence suggests a diversity of developments. The Wall Street Journal has reported that the labor force near the Mexican border lacks the skills required by manufacturers moving in to produce parts for nearby Mexican assembly plants (Cooper 1997). These manufacturers must recruit outside the region. Many new meat-processing plants in the Great Plains states pay such low wages that they, too, must recruit outside their local labor markets, but for unskilled workers (Broadway 1994). Urban stockbrokers and other highly educated providers of producer services are moving to rural areas, using phone, fax, and electronic and express mail to serve their clients (Beyers and Lindahl 1996). At the same time, financial and insurance companies are establishing rural "back offices" to do low-skill clerical work. Although a wide variety of changes are occurring across rural regions of the country, broad forces are nonetheless constraining the kinds of activities that develop in and move to rural areas, thereby shaping rural opportunities and the context for economic development policy. This chapter reports our research into these broad forces as they affected job creation, population migration, and changes in earnings during the early 1990's.

Much of this analysis is an update of our study of education demand and supply trends in rural and urban areas during the 1980's (McGranahan and Ghelfi 1991).[1] Demand for worker education and skills rose during the 1980's, while young adults were completing fewer years of college, raising questions as to whether the United States could compete internationally without substantially upgrading its workforce or allowing real wages to fall. And earnings did fall, particularly for less educated workers.

This "education crisis" was accompanied by a rural crisis marked by high unemployment, weak employment growth, declining earnings relative to urban, and net outmigration to urban areas. We found two sources of the rural economic problems of the 1980's. First, the heavily rural production sector industries— agriculture, mining, and routine manufacturing—lost employment during the 1980's. Second, rural areas did not maintain their share of faster growing industries or of high-education production sector jobs. We found no evidence that lack of supply of highly educated workers in rural areas was behind these two rural trends. Rural education levels had been even lower relative to urban levels in 1970, but rural areas experienced higher growth in high-education production sector jobs than urban areas in the 1970's. During the 1980's, the premium paid to young adults for higher education levels rose much faster in urban than in rural areas, suggesting that the increase in demand for better educated workers was disproportionately urban. Finally, a relatively high proportion of better educated rural residents migrated to urban areas. Our conclusion was that rural economic problems in the 1980's stemmed from lack of employer demand, particularly for highly educated workers. The rural regions of the country did not seem to be participating in the "New Economy," with its new technology and shift toward higher skilled jobs.

In the 1990's, earnings inequality between low- and high-education workers has continued to increase nationally, suggesting a continued shortage of better educated workers relative to demand as well as a continued decline in the effects of unions on wages (Mishel et al. 1997). But the strength of the U.S. economy, with the lowest unemployment rate since the 1970's, has blunted immediate concerns about U.S. competitiveness. And, although rural earnings remain considerably below urban earnings, rural unemployment is low, and more people are moving into than out of rural areas, blunting concerns about rural competitiveness. In this chapter, we examine job trends in the 1990's as they affect the need for high- and low-education workers, educational trends among the workforce-age population, rural-urban migration, and rural and urban trends in earnings by education, all with a view toward understanding how conditions have changed in the 1990's and what these changes mean for rural development policy, particularly in the area of education and training.

THE RURAL ROLE IN THE NATIONAL ECONOMY

An understanding of the patterns of rural (and urban) job creation requires some knowledge of the spatial organization of the economy. Rural and urban people have quite different roles in the national economy, and changes in the national economy may have different consequences for their economic livelihoods. In our earlier study, drawing on the concept of economic base, we delineated the production sector from the consumer services sector. Broadly, the production sector is concerned with the production of goods and services that are exported from a region or areas; this is the activity upon which the local economy depends for bringing in outside income. Included in this sector are agriculture, mining, manufacturing, and producer services—financial, legal, accounting, and other activities upon which the rest of the production sector depends. The production sector is organized nationally and increasingly internationally, with regions and nations attempting to develop and maintain niches.

The consumer services sector is largely concerned with the activities that serve the local population, and its products usually are not exported outside of the local area. Organized in trade or service areas, consumer services depend on the vitality and growth of the production sector. We included distributional (transportation, communication, utilities, and wholesale trade), retail, and personal services; health, education, and professional services; government; and construction industries in the consumer services sector. Since households everywhere have many of the same needs, and most of these needs are met locally, these industries are pervasive and largely proportional to population.[2]

In 1995, about one-third of urban (metro) employment was in production sector jobs and two-thirds in consumer services sector jobs (Table 8.1). Rural (nonmetro) employment was more heavily concentrated in production sector jobs than urban employment, but the difference was only slight. Within the production sector, urban and rural areas have markedly different niches. About 27 percent of urban employment in this sector was in agriculture, mining, and routine manufacturing—traditionally low-wage, low-skill industries, and 73 percent in complex manufacturing and producer services—industry groups with high proportions of managers and professionals. In contrast, nearly 60 percent of rural employment was in the low-skill group, while only 40 percent was in the high-skill industries. The index of dissimilarity (the percentage of rural jobs that would have to move from one industry to another to equalize the rural and urban proportions in each industry) was 32 percent. This is higher than the 28.1 percent we reported for 1980, reflecting the increasing concentration of high-skill industries into urban areas during the 1980's (McGranahan and Ghelfi 1991).

In contrast to the very disparate production sector activities found in urban and rural areas, consumer services sector activities are quite similar. Compared with the urban consumer services sector, the rural sector has somewhat lower proportions in the distribution industries and in health, education, and profes-

TABLE **8.1.** Distribution of jobs in urban and rural areas by sector

Sector and industry group	1989			1995	
	Urban	Rural		Urban	Rural
			Percent		
Production sector					
Agriculture, forestry, and fishing	3.2	15.1		2.8	14.8
Mining	1.3	4.4		0.9	3.5
Routine manufacturing	25.0	41.3		23.3	40.7
Complex manufacturing	25.2	16.7		23.5	16.0
Producer services	45.3	22.6		49.5	25.0
Total	100.0	100.0		100.0	100.0
Share of total area jobs	33.1	36.6		32.2	35.4
Consumer services sector					
Distribution[a]	17.2	14.2		15.6	13.7
Retail and personal	36.5	39.0		38.4	40.4
Health, education, and professional	29.6	28.2		29.9	28.0
Government	7.1	6.9		6.8	6.8
Construction	9.6	11.8		9.3	11.2
Total	100.0	100.0		100.0	100.0
Share of total area jobs	66.9	63.4		67.8	64.6
Index of urban-rural dissimilarity					
Production sector	...	31.2		...	32.0
Consumer services sector	...	4.6		...	3.8

[a]Includes transportation, communications, utilities, and wholesale trade.
Source: Calculated by the authors using data from the 1990 Census of Population and the March 1996 Current Population Survey files.

sional services, but a higher proportion in retail and personal services. This reflects the fact that most major institutions (e.g., teaching hospitals, research universities, and international communications firms) in the distributive and professional service industries are located in urban centers. But, overall, differences in the consumer services sector are relatively small, as reflected in the very small index of dissimilarity for 1995 of 3.8 percent, which is about the same as we found in 1980 (4.1 percent).

The distinct rural industrial structure captures only some of the differences in economic activities between rural and urban areas. Within production sector industries, rural areas tend to specialize in production jobs while urban areas specialize in management and research (McGranahan 1988). In 1995, for instance, 25 percent of urban manufacturing jobs were in management and professional jobs, compared with 10 percent of rural manufacturing jobs (Table 8.2). And 80 percent of rural manufacturing jobs were production jobs, compared with 58 percent in urban areas. These differences reflect not only differences in industrial composition but also the tendency for firms to locate headquarters and research and development labs in urban areas while more routine production jobs are located in rural plants.

Broadly, the rural and urban parts of the economy have become more similar over time, at least as measured by employment. Employment in the consumer services sector has grown more rapidly than employment in the production sector, in part because productivity gains have been greater in the production sector and in part because consumers are now purchasing many of the services that used to be done in the household—people are eating out more, for example. Since the consumer services sector is quite similar in rural and urban areas, its expansion has tended to reduce overall rural-urban differences in industrial structure. However, neither in the 1980's nor thus far in the 1990's has there been any decrease in the rural-urban division of labor in the production sector. Indeed, in the 1980's, differences increased markedly. In the 1990's, at least as measured by the index of dissimilarity, there has been little change.

RURAL-URBAN DIFFERENCES IN THE EDUCATIONAL REQUIREMENTS OF JOBS

The differences in the industrial and occupational mixes of rural and urban jobs suggest that rural jobs generally have much lower educational requirements than urban jobs. To directly assess these differences, we used microdata from the

TABLE 8.2. Occupational distribution and change in manufacturing jobs

Area type and occupational group	Percent distribution		Percent change in jobs	
	1989	1995	1990-96	1980-88
Urban				
Managerial and professional	21.2	25.0	13.8	34.5
Support, other white collar	20.8	17.4	-19.1	-6.0
Production worker[a]	58.0	57.7	-3.9	-12.6
Total	100.0	100.0	-3.3	-3.5
Rural				
Managerial and professional	8.7	9.5	9.4	-0.8
Support, other white collar	12.5	10.8	-13.7	-6.0
Production worker[a]	78.8	79.7	1.2	1.7
Total	100.0	100.0	0.0	0.5

[a]Includes production and service jobs.
Source: Calculated by the authors using data from the 1980 and 1990 Censuses of Population Public Use Microdata Files and the 1987, 1988, and 1996 March Current Population Survey files.

1990 Census of Population to calculate the educational levels of full-time, full-year workers in 1989 in each of 443 industry/occupation categories at the national level.[3] We then used these levels as standards to assess the educational "requirements" of jobs held by all rural and urban workers in 1989. This is the same method and categorization that we used to assess educational requirements in 1980, except we used the industry and occupation of the current job rather than of the longest job held in 1979. The nearly identical methods in our analyses allow a comparison of results in the two decades.

Overall, urban jobs had higher educational needs than rural jobs in 1989. About 25 percent of urban jobs typically required at least a college degree, compared with only 18 percent of rural jobs (Table 8.3). About 45 percent of urban jobs required no more than a high school diploma, compared with 53 percent of rural jobs.

In the production sector, where most of the rural-urban differences in occupation and industry are found, the rural-urban differences in job educational requirements were quite pronounced. About 24 percent of urban jobs in this sector were typically college level or above, but only 13 percent of rural production jobs required that much education. And while 12 percent of urban production sector jobs were low-education jobs, 20 percent of the rural jobs did not require a high school diploma. Rural-urban differences in the consumer services sector are relatively minor, as reflected in the small index of dissimilarity.

The low educational requirements of rural jobs reflect the spatial structure of the economy but do not explain the structure. In fact, our analysis of trends in the 1980's strongly suggested that the spatial organization of the economy was more a cause than a result of low rural education levels and that limited rural demand for more highly educated workers is a major reason for the spatial structure (McGranahan and Ghelfi 1991). But the 1990's are a different context. The

TABLE 8.3. Percent distribution of jobs by educational requirements, 1989

Area and sector	No HS diploma	HS diploma	Some college	BA/BS degree	Higher degree	Total	Index of urban-rural dissimilarity
Urban							
Production	11.7	34.2	29.8	17.2	7.1	100.0	...
Consumer services	10.7	33.8	30.9	15.2	9.3	100.0	...
Total	11.0	34.0	30.5	15.9	8.6	100.0	...
Rural							
Production	19.8	42.1	25.0	10.0	3.2	100.0	16.0
Consumer services	12.5	36.0	30.1	13.5	8.0	100.0	3.9
Total	15.2	38.2	28.2	12.2	6.2	100.0	8.4

Source: Calculated by the authors using data from the 1990 Census of Population Public Use Microdata file.

1980–82 recessions were led by problems in routine manufacturing, mining, and agriculture (more rural industries), while defense, computer, and financial industries (more urban, high-education industries) boomed. The 1990–91 recession was led by shrinkage in the defense budget, a shakedown in the computer industry, and a faltering of the financial services and business real estate industries. Caught off guard in the 1980's by cheap imports, many industries have restructured and, with the help of a weaker dollar and new technologies, become more competitive. To look into the effects of these more recent industrial trends, we next examine changes in the educational requirements of jobs related to changes in the occupational/industrial mix.

CHANGES IN EDUCATIONAL REQUIREMENTS RESULTING FROM CHANGES IN JOB MIX

Changes in the skill requirements of jobs can be thought of as comprising two types of change: change in the industrial and occupational mix of jobs (e.g., growing proportions of bankers and lawyers would raise skill requirements while growing proportions of retail clerks would lower skill requirements) and changes in the skill content of individual jobs over time (e.g., introducing new technology could either raise or lower the skills needed to do a job depending on whether the new equipment makes the job more difficult or easier). The pervasive adoption of the computer illustrates how these two types of changes often occur together. For instance, personal computers in the office environment have reduced the proportion of secretaries in the workforce while simultaneously raising the skills required of those who remain.

Changes in skill requirements are related to changes in educational requirements, but as we saw in the previous chapter, the linkage is not complete. Required skills may or may not be learned as part of the normal school experience, although it is certainly arguable that part of the importance of schooling is that it makes one more able to learn new skills. Our analysis of changes in educational requirements stemming from changes in the industry/occupation mix of jobs thus gives a partial picture of the changing demand for skills.

In our analysis of the 1970's and 1980's, we found considerable shifts in jobs towards higher education requirements—as others did (Levy 1987; Burtless 1990). While the overall shift toward high-education jobs was slightly stronger in the 1970's than 1980's, the production sector shift, where increasing international competition and technological change probably played large roles, was much greater in the 1980's than in the 1970's (Figure 8.1). This was offset by a much reduced shift toward high-education jobs in the consumer services sector. Growth in health, education, and professional services and government—industry groups with relatively high education levels—was slower in the 1980's than in the previous decade. At the same time, growth accelerated in the 1980's in retail and personal services, both low-education industries.

Thus far in the 1990's, the overall growth in the number of jobs has been less than it was in the previous two decades, largely because the baby boom generation, which had fueled job growth in the 1970's and 1980's, is already in the labor market and the subsequent cohort of new labor force entrants has been relatively small. The slowing in employment growth was accompanied by a considerable slowdown in the shift toward high-education jobs.

While a lack of new labor force entrants may have limited the shift toward high-education jobs, what was quite new to the 1990's was an apparent growth in jobs typically going to those without a high school degree, at a rate that exceeded the growth in jobs for those with a high school diploma or even those with some college (Table 8.4)[4]. This pattern was evident in the retail/personal services and producer services industry groups in the 1980's but became more pronounced and more widespread in the 1990's, when it appeared in agriculture, manufacturing, and distributive services. In producer services, the jobs typically occupied by workers lacking a high school diploma grew faster than the jobs for any of the other education groups in the 1990's (See appendix tables 8.1 and 8.2).

Possible explanations for these shifts toward low- as well as high-end jobs occur on both the demand and supply side. On the demand side, changes in technology, particularly the introduction of the personal computer, appear to have reduced midrange jobs (e.g., draftspersons, technical workers, designers, secretaries) more than others.[5] This is particularly evident in manufacturing, where professional and managerial jobs increased, technical, sales, and administrative support jobs declined considerably, and production jobs remained fairly stable after a sharp decline in the 1980's (Table 8.2). On the supply side, the influx of

FIGURE 8.1. Change in average education level of national jobs by industrial sector, at 10-year rates

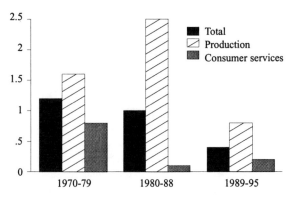

Source: Calculated by the authors using data from the 1970, 1980, and 1990 Censuses of population public use microdata files and the March 1979, 1988, and 1997 Current Population Survey files.

TABLE 8.4. Percent change in number of workers by job education levels (10-year rates)

Period, type of area, and sector	No HS diploma	HS diploma	Some college	College degree	Beyond college	Total
1989-95						
National						
Production	4.5	0.7	3.8	17.5	18.6	5.8
Consumer services	14.2	12.4	13.4	14.2	18.9	13.7
Total	10.4	8.2	10.2	15.4	18.8	11.0
Urban						
Production	5.7	0.0	3.7	18.5	20.1	6.2
Consumer services	14.7	12.5	13.0	13.9	19.4	13.7
Total	11.6	8.3	10.0	15.4	19.5	11.2
Rural						
Production	1.5	2.7	4.2	11.2	5.2	3.7
Consumer services	11.9	11.9	14.9	16.5	16.2	13.9
Total	6.9	8.1	11.4	14.9	14.0	10.0
1980-88						
National						
Production	1.4	9.6	26.3	46.1	56.5	17.1
Consumer services	30.9	29.7	30.8	32.7	31.1	30.6
Total	17.9	21.7	29.3	37.7	38.1	25.4
Urban						
Production	0.7	11.5	31.1	53.3	63.2	20.9
Consumer services	33.9	31.5	32.5	34.8	32.8	32.6
Total	20.1	23.7	31.9	41.9	41.6	28.2
Rural						
Production	3.1	3.8	7.3	10.4	16.9	5.1
Consumer services	20.6	22.9	24.3	24.0	24.0	22.9
Total	11.6	14.7	18.4	19.4	22.3	15.5

Source: Calculated by the authors using data from the 1980 and 1990 Censuses of Population Public Use Microdata files and the 1987, 1988, and 1996 March Current Population Survey files.

Latin American and other immigrants has increased the number of young people available for low-end jobs, at least in major urban areas. As shown later in the chapter, the wages for workers without a high school diploma have declined considerably in real terms over the past 20 years, particularly for young adults, ages 18–34. This may have made it more attractive to organize production around these workers. It seems unlikely, however, that supply was the dominant factor. As we shall see later, the number of working-age people without a high school degree has been declining substantially, despite immigration. Many of these low-education jobs may have been upgraded as they were filled with people with at least high school degrees.

Gains in the educational levels of jobs have been quite uneven over time, with respect to both industry sector and geography. During the 1970's, the shift to high-education jobs was particularly rapid, probably facilitated by the high education levels and large size of the leading edge of the baby boom generation and the decline in the premium paid for highly educated workers. Rural employment grew more rapidly than urban employment during this period, and our analysis shows that rural gains in the educational levels of jobs were greater than urban gains (Figure 8.2). During the 1980's, employment growth slowed, and the educational level of young adults (ages 25–34) declined. The growth in job educational levels continued but at a much reduced rate with the major exception of the urban production sector, where the gain nearly doubled from the previous decade. Where the gain in job education levels in the 1970's was facilitated by the increase in supply, the gain in the 1980's appears to have been demand driven, as it was associated with a substantial increase in the urban premium paid to highly educated workers, particularly young adults.

While some of the urban concentration of high-education jobs in the 1980–88 period reflected the relatively large share of producer services in urban areas and the rapid growth in those services nationally over the decade, some of the concentration reflected a shift of professional and managerial functions from rural to urban areas. In manufacturing, managerial and professional jobs increased by a third in urban areas over the decade but did not increase at all in rural areas. At the same time, rural areas increased their share of manufacturing production jobs, largely because the decline in these jobs was confined to metro areas (Table 8.2).

In the 1990's, the rate of gain in the education level of jobs has slowed in both

FIGURE 8.2. Change in average education levels of rural and urban jobs by industrial sector, at 10-year intervals

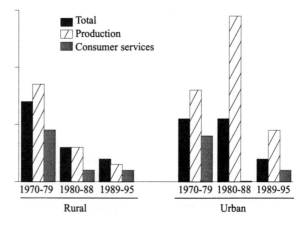

Source: Calculated by the authors using data from the 1970, 1980, and 1990 Censuses of Population Public Use Microdata files and the March 1979, 1988, and 1997 Current Population Survey files.

the urban and rural production sectors, but particularly the urban production sector (although the gain in education level remains highest in that sector). Jobs for the least as well as the most educated have been expanding at the expense of the jobs for people with high school diplomas or some college but no college degree. It is in urban areas, particularly in the production sector, that the development of this J-shaped pattern is most pronounced (Table 8.4).

In rural areas, the shift toward higher-education jobs continues to be largely monotonic—the higher the educational category, the greater the increase in jobs. At the top end, however, jobs typically filled by people with higher degrees have grown at about the same rate as for those with a BA degree only. Overall in 1990–96, the jobs for both the most and least educated are now growing more rapidly in urban areas than in rural areas, not just the college-level and above jobs, as was true of the 1980–88 period. As with most patterns, this is most pronounced in the production sector.

A Shift-Share Analysis

The continued tendency for high-education jobs to grow somewhat more rapidly in urban than rural areas may stem from one or a combination of two sources. First, it may reflect the different industrial/occupational compositions of urban and rural areas and the differential growth rates of those industries and jobs. Urban types of high-education jobs may be growing more rapidly than the rural types, for instance. Second, employers may be continuing the shift of high-education jobs to urban areas that began in the 1980's, if at a reduced rate. To the extent that the latter is the case, it suggests that rurality itself remains an impediment in local competition for high-education jobs.

To explore this issue, we used a simple shift/share analysis. We applied national growth rates to nonmetro employment in the 443 industry/occupation groups to calculate expected nonmetro growth rates on the basis of the nonmetro "shares" of the various industry/occupation groups. The difference between the actual and expected rates then represent the geographic "shifts" in jobs between rural and urban areas—changes in employment that exceed or fall short of what would have happened if growth rates had been the same in rural and urban areas (see Appendix I for a more detailed explanation of our methods).

The results show that both the strong centralization of production sector high-education jobs in urban areas and the decentralization of low-education jobs in rural areas that characterized the 1980's have largely abated in the 1990's (Table 8.5). Overall, there was relatively little shifting of jobs in 1989–95 compared with a decade earlier. Rural areas still gain slightly more production sector jobs than expected on the basis of national growth rates, but they are more the middle range jobs than the low-education jobs. The fact that high-education jobs have grown more rapidly in urban than rural areas during this decade is due entirely to the faster growth of those types of jobs that were most concentrated in urban areas at the beginning of the decade.

Some of the factors that may have been behind the centralization in the 1980's appear to have weakened. First, producers are facing less uncertainty—less need for access to specialized information and knowledge about technology and markets. According to product-cycle theory and its variants, economic activities decentralize out of urban areas when technology and markets are routinized (Malecki 1991). Rapid, face-to-face access to information and specialized knowledge are less critical to success. However, the 1980's was a period of new uncertainties in both technology—with the introduction of microchip-based technology—and markets—with trade globalization and competition from imports. According to a recent study using an input-output framework, jobs generated by manufacturing exports were about the same as jobs "lost" through imports in 1982, each amounting to about 19 percent of all jobs generated by manufacturing (Lee and Hanson 1997). By 1987, manufacturing exports accounted for fewer jobs, down to 17 percent of jobs generated by manufacturing. But manufacturing imports rose by 88 percent and, had they been produced in the country, would have created 26 percent more jobs than manufacturing was generating, a considerable encroachment into the U.S. market. Many U.S. producers moved plants abroad during this period. Since the mid-1980's, however, the trade-weighted exchange rate has fallen by about 35 percent, easing competitive pressures from abroad. Imports have risen, but far less rapidly than exports, which now account for 27 percent of the jobs generated by manufacturing.

Competitive pressures spurred many manufacturers to adopt new technologies and new forms of work organization designed to save labor costs and, especially, improve quality. These technologies themselves may now have become routinized. They have been widely adopted in rural areas, and what little gap in technology use remains can be explained by the rural mix of industries (Gale 1997). Calmer, more certain markets and better understood production technologies, perhaps combined with the greater use of new telecommunications technologies, appear to have reduced uncertainty and dampened the need for immediate access to information and specialized services. The location of management and professional activities in a major urban area may no longer be such an advantage. There is as yet little indication of decentralization, however.

A second factor that may have reduced centralization tendencies may have been a decline in the rate of development of branch plants abroad. The rapid growth in urban managerial and professional jobs may have stemmed partly from the globalization of corporations during the 1980's, with headquarters in the United States, but an increasing proportion of production carried out in overseas plants often located in countries with low labor costs. The pace of this globalization appears to have slowed down, perhaps in part due to changes in exchange rates and the increasing efficiency of U.S. plants. Finally, the industries that faltered in the early 1990's were urban, high-education industries, most notably defense and finance, the very industries whose growth fueled urban economies during the 1980's. In sum, while the New Economy was clearly an urban econo-

TABLE 8.5. Components of changes in jobs by educational requirements (10-year rates)

| Industry sector and job education requirements | 1989-95 | | | | 1980-88 |
| | Urban | Rural | | | Rural |
	Actual change	Actual change	Expected change	Actual-expected	Actual-expected
			Percent		
Total					
No HS diploma	11.6	6.9	8.0	-1.0	-1.2
HS diploma	8.3	8.1	7.4	0.7	-2.9
Some college	10.0	11.4	9.7	1.7	-7.5
BA degree	15.4	14.9	12.8	2.1	-13
Graduate degree	19.5	14	15.1	-1.1	-9.9
Total	11.2	10	9.3	0.7	-4.6
Production sector					
No HS diploma	5.7	1.5	1.3	0.2	11.1
HS diploma	0.0	2.7	-0.8	3.5	6.7
Some college	3.7	4.2	-0.3	4.5	-3.7
BA degree	18.5	11.2	7.1	4.1	-17.7
Graduate degree	20.1	5.2	8.0	-2.7	-21.7
Total	6.2	3.7	0.8	2.9	3.6
Consumer services sector					
No HS diploma	14.7	11.9	14.2	-2.3	-13.5
HS diploma	12.5	11.9	13.2	-1.2	-10.1
Some college	13	14.9	14.7	0.2	-9.6
BA degree	13.9	16.5	15.4	1.1	-10.7
Graduate degree	19.4	16.2	16.9	-0.7	-6.5
Total	13.7	13.9	14.4	-0.5	-10.4

Source: Calculated by the authors using data from the 1980 and 1990 Censuses of Population Public Use Microdata files and the 1987, 1988, and 1996 March Current Population Survey files.

my in the 1980's, this is much less true in the 1990's. Rural manufacturers have adopted new technologies and, aided by a weaker dollar, increased their competitiveness in international markets.

EDUCATION LEVELS OF THE POPULATION

The education levels of the working-age (ages 18–64) population have risen considerably over the past three decades, but at diminishing rates. The number without a high school diploma or equivalent has decreased at a rate of about 25 percent a decade in each of the three periods (Table 8.6). However, the numbers with some college, BA/BS degrees, or higher degrees, which had increased at astounding rates during the 1970's (a reflection of the high rate of college and postcollege attendance during the Vietnam war), have increased at lower rates in each succeeding decade. In part, this reflects the slower growth in the young adult population in recent decades as the baby boom generation aged and was succeeded by a relatively small cohort. Even though lower than in earlier periods, the rates of growth in the populations with BA/BS and higher degrees were 44 and 24 percent per decade in the 1990–96 period, four times and twice the rate of growth of the working-age population as a whole.

These gains in the education levels of the workforce are considerably greater than the measured gains in the educational requirements of jobs. It cannot be inferred, however, that there is now an excess of better educated workers. As noted above, our measure of changes in educational requirements reflects only shifts stemming from changes in the industrial/occupational mix of jobs. New technology or quality needs also affect the educational requirements of individual jobs, and it is not possible to directly assess this type of change in educational requirements. The analysis in the previous chapter suggests that the change in job content has been substantial, at least in manufacturing, in the past decade.

Rural-Urban Differences

The rural working-age population has considerably less education than the urban working-age population. Nearly 19 percent of the rural working-age population did not have a high school diploma (or equivalent) in 1996 (Table 8.6). Only 14 percent had at least a college degree. In contrast, the urban proportion without a high school diploma was significantly lower (15 percent), while the proportion with a college degree or more was nearly twice as high (25 percent) as in rural areas.

The rural-urban difference in the proportion with a high school degree is to some extent an historical legacy. Among young adults (ages 25–34), the differences are much smaller—about 14 percent in rural areas lack a high school degree compared with 13 percent in urban areas (Table 8.7). While the number of rural dropouts is still significant, rural education systems have improved more than urban systems, at least in terms of preventing dropouts (see Chapter 3). Moreover, with some exceptions, rural areas have received less than their share of recent low-education immigrants. In both the 1980's and the 1990's, the population lacking a high school diploma has declined more rapidly in rural than urban areas.

The differences in the proportion of the working-age population with a college degree or more stem from both a greater tendency for rural high school graduates not to go on to college and from the substantial outmigration of the more highly educated young adults from rural to urban areas during the 1980's (see Chapter 4 and McGranahan and Ghelfi 1991). The proportion of the rural working-age population with a college degree or more was only 3 percentage points higher in 1996 than it had been in 1980. In contrast, the urban proportion

TABLE 8.6. Education attained by the population ages 18-64

	1996		Change (10-year rate)		
			1990-96	1980-88	1970-79
	Millions	*Percent distribution*		*Percent*	
National					
No diploma	25.3	15.7	-25.2	-24.7	-26.1
HS diploma	53.4	33.0	26.0	18.7	37.4
Some college	45.6	28.3	3.8	21.6	58.9
BA degree	25.5	15.8	43.6	76.0	86.5
Higher degree	11.6	7.2	23.9	32.6	80.4
Total	161.5	100.0	10.6	12.9	20.1
Urban					
No diploma	19.7	15.0	-24.0	-23.2	...
HS diploma	41.0	31.3	26.5	18.8	...
Some college	37.6	28.6	2.3	23.4	...
BA degree	22.6	17.2	44.7	85.0	...
Higher degree	10.3	7.9	24.3	32.9	...
Total	131.2	100.0	11.3	15.9	...
Rural					
No diploma	5.7	18.8	-28.8	-28.8	...
HS diploma	12.4	40.7	24.1	18.3	...
Some college	8.1	26.6	11.2	13.7	...
BA degree	2.9	9.7	35.3	31.2	...
Higher degree	1.3	4.3	21.2	31.4	...
Total	30.4	100.0	7.8	3.2	...

Source: Calculated by the authors using data from the 1970, 1980, and 1990 Censuses of Population Public Use Microdata files and the March 1979, 1987, 1988, and 1996 Current Population Survey files.

was 9 percentage points higher than in 1980. This increasing metro concentration is also reflected in the population ages 25–34, in which the rural-urban gap in the proportion with a BA or higher degree (13.1 percent) is even larger than among the working-age population as a whole (11.1 percent).

The concentration of more highly educated people in urban areas has continued in the 1990's, but at a much reduced rate. The 10-year rate of growth in urban college graduates fell from 85 percent in the 1980's to 45 percent in the 1990's. In contrast, the rate of growth in rural college graduates rose from 31 percent in 1980–88 to 35 percent in 1990-96. (The growth rates in the postgraduate population declined in both urban and rural areas from about 30 percent to 20 percent between the two decades, still substantial rates of increase.) This suggests that the urban pull was weaker in the 1990's than in the previous decade, which is quite

TABLE **8.7.** Percent distributions of young adults, ages 25-34, by educational attainment, 1996

Education attained	National	Urban	Rural
No HS diploma	13.1	12.9	14.2
HS diploma to some college	60.4	58.4	70.1
BA/BS degree or higher degree	26.5	28.7	15.6
Total	100.0	100.0	100.0

Source: Calculated by the authors using data from the March 1996 Current Population Survey.

consistent with the changes noted earlier in the relative growth rates in the educational requirements of jobs in rural and urban areas.

Comparing Supply and Demand for Education

The working-age population in rural areas has relatively low education levels compared with the urban population, but we also know that the educational requirements of rural jobs are relatively low. To assess whether rural areas have an education shortage or surplus compared with requirements, we computed both the proportion of jobs and the proportion of working population at three education levels that were in rural areas in 1996. The results suggest that, compared with educational requirements, rural areas have both relatively few workers lacking a high school degree and relatively few college graduates (Table 8.8). The differences are greater for young adults (ages 25–34) than the working-age population as a whole and tend to be greater in the production sector than in the consumer services sector. While 12 percent of the production sector jobs that are typically filled by college graduates are located in rural areas, rural areas have only 9 percent of college graduates who had worked at all in that sector during the previous year. Among young adults, the proportion who had worked in the sector is less than 8 percent. There is also a shortfall in the consumer services sector. Conversely, it appears that rural employers are more able to find high school graduates and those with some college for medium-skill jobs, perhaps a motivation for locating in rural areas.[6]

RURAL-URBAN MIGRATION

Migration rates between rural and urban areas shed further light on the rural education shortage/surplus issue. These rates show markedly different patterns in the four-year period up to the 1990–91 recession and the subsequent four years, suggesting that 1991 was a watershed event for the geography of development. The 1980–82 recessions a decade earlier marked the beginning of the concentration of high-education activities into urban areas and the beginning of a rural "brain drain," with a substantial outflow of more highly educated working-age people. The 1990–91 recession marked the end of that brain drain, at least until present. From 1987 to 1991, rural areas had a net loss of college-educated working-age people each year that averaged about 1.3 percent per year, a substantial cumulative loss, especially since migration is heaviest among young adults (Table 8.9).[7] This outflow ceased in 1991–92, and since 1991, rural areas have had a small net inflow of this highly educated population each year, averaging about a half a percent per year.

Between 1987 and 1991, rural areas gained residents who lacked a high school degree at the rate of about 1 percent per year, a trend that continued into the 1990's. Since the working-age population lacking a high school diploma has been falling more rapidly in rural than urban areas, this suggests that the negative effects of the inflow of low-education immigrants from abroad on urban education levels have been somewhat blunted by the outflow of U.S.-born low-education population to rural areas.

In sum, the migration data are consistent with the supply/demand analysis presented above in suggesting that rural areas, despite the J-shape of the growth of urban jobs by education level, have relatively greater opportunities for both dropouts and college graduates, opportunities that have been inducing or allowing them to move to rural areas.

EDUCATION AND REAL EARNINGS

Changes in real earnings over the past 20 years have reflected changes in the supply and demand for workforce education. Nationally, during the 1980's, average annual earnings fell for full-time, full-year workers without a high school

TABLE 8.8. Rural jobs and workforce as percents of national totals by education level, 1995

	Total			Production sector			Consumer services		
		Workforce[a]			Workforce[a]			Workforce[a]	
Education level	Jobs	Ages 18-64	Ages 25-34	Jobs	Ages 18-64	Ages 25-34	Jobs	Ages 18-64	Ages 25-34
No HS diploma	23.6	22.7	19.7	29.6	26.3	22.8	20.0	20.7	17.8
HS diploma	19.2	20.7	20.0	21.2	23.3	22.0	18.2	19.4	18.9
BA degree	14.6	11.5	10.1	11.6	8.8	7.9	16.0	12.8	11.3
Total	18.6	18.6	17.2	20.0	20.0	18.2	17.9	17.9	16.6

[a]People who worked at all during 1995.
Source: Calculated by the authors using data from the March 1996 Current Population Survey.

diploma but rose slightly for workers with a BA/BS or higher degree (Table 8.10). Among young adults, who are most directly affected by labor market shifts, college graduates in the production sector had the greatest gains in earnings, even though their earnings were already 20 percent higher than their counterparts' in the consumer services sector at the start of the decade. This is consistent with the extraordinarily strong rise in the educational requirements of production sector jobs in the 1980's.

In the 1989–95 period, earnings trends have still depended on education, but less markedly than in the 1980's. While real earnings declined at about the same rate for working-age high school dropouts in both periods, earnings declined more sharply for the high school graduate to some college group in 1989–95 than in 1978–89. Among younger earners, the fall in earnings matched that of high school dropouts, perhaps a reflection of the relative lack of job growth for high school graduates. Earnings of college graduates have fallen slightly in this decade, although changes in Current Population Survey methodology and topcoding of the highest earnings make comparisons for this group somewhat difficult to evaluate.[9]

Complex changes in earnings patterns over time, between rural and urban areas, between the production sector and the consumer services sector, and across education groups are summarized in Table 8.11. In this table, average earnings of full-time, full-year workers in each residence/industry sector/education group in each age group in each year are expressed as a percentage of the national average earnings of all full-time, full-year workers in the age group and year. Briefly, these data show the following trends:

1. The earnings of rural workers declined relative to the national average as the economy became more urban between 1978 and 1989 and rose as urbanization forces eased between 1989 and 1995. This pattern was stronger among younger than all workers. Average earnings for younger rural workers went from 92 percent of the national average in 1978 to 80 percent in 1989 and up to 85 percent in 1995.

2. The rise in the relative earnings of young, high-education, production sector workers between 1978 and 1989 was confined entirely to urban areas. Their

TABLE 8.9. Average annual percent change in the rural population ages 25 to 64 due to net migration

Education level	1987-91	1991-96
No HS diploma	0.96	0.95
HS diploma through some college	0.08	0.10
BA/BS degree or higher degree	-1.32	0.51

Source: Calculated by the authors using data from the March 1987-96 Current Population Survey files.

rural counterparts actually lost substantial ground during that period, reflecting the relative decline in their opportunities, particularly in the production sector. Other rural education groups also lost ground in the 1980's as the rural economy sagged, but the rural-urban earnings gap was largest among college graduates in 1989, with urban young adults in the production sector earning a third again as much as their rural counterparts.

3. Although there was relative stability in the earnings of both urban and rural college graduates as a whole between 1989 and 1995, rural young adults in the group saw their earnings rise markedly, particularly in the production sector.[8] This is another indicator that the forces that increasingly concentrated management, professional, and other high-education jobs in urban areas have abated during the 1990's and is consistent with the reversal in the rural-urban migration pattern of this education group.

4. The middle education group, those with a high school diploma to some college, lost ground in both rural and urban areas in the 1978–89 period, but the rural loss was more substantial in both sectors and in both age groups. In the 1989–95 period, however, the loss in relative position was entirely urban, consistent with the relatively slow growth in urban jobs for this group. In rural areas, the middle education group has had slight gains in the 1990's, more among young adults than the working-age population as a whole. Urban earnings remain substantially above rural earnings, however, for this education group in both industrial sectors.

5. The decline in earnings among workers without a high school diploma was ubiquitous in the 1978–89 period, occurring in both industrial sectors, in rural and urban areas, and in both age groups. From 1989 to 1995, however, the decline was almost entirely urban and resulted in near earnings parity between rural and urban low-education workers. Since the cost of housing is generally lower in rural areas, low-education workers are probably now economically better off in rural than urban areas, at least those workers who can find full-time jobs. This is consistent with the outmigration of this group from urban to rural areas during this period.

CONCLUSION

Rural areas play a distinct role in the national economy, particularly in the production sector. In general, they specialize in agriculture, mining, and routine manufacturing and, within these industries, they specialize in production rather than management and research. This specialization is shaped in part by the small size and remoteness of rural communities. Those characteristics limit rural activities in several ways, including the ability to develop highly technical, diverse sets of activities and corresponding workforces. In general, this limitation does not appear to have been shaped by the quality of rural labor.

But the degree to which rural areas specialize in low-education activities is not

TABLE 8.10. Average annual earnings for full-time, full-year workers by age, industry sector, and education

	1978	1989	1995	1978-89	1989-95
				\<Change\>	
		1995 dollars		*Percent*	
Ages 18-64	32,655	33,272	32,690	1.9	-1.8
Consumer services sector	31,344	31,439	31,050	0.3	-1.2
No HS diploma	24,837	21,688	20,119	-12.7	-7.2
HS diploma to some college	28,738	28,042	27,034	-2.4	-3.6
BA/BS or higher degree	41,998	42,808	42,910	1.9	0.2
Production sector	34,308	35,975	35,292	4.9	-1.9
No HS diploma	26,151	22,670	20,400	-13.3	-10.0
HS diploma to some college	31,983	31,393	30,204	-1.8	-3.8
BA/BS or higher degree	52,497	53,397	52,305	1.7	-2.0
Ages 18-34	27,906	27,386	26,020	-1.9	-5.0
Consumer services sector	27,013	25,911	24,624	-4.1	-5.0
No HS diploma	21,719	18,193	16,893	-16.2	-7.1
HS diploma to some college	25,058	24,047	22,179	-4.0	-7.8
BA/BS or higher degree	33,628	34,188	33,503	1.7	-2.0
Production sector	29,057	29,590	28,282	1.8	-4.4
No HS diploma	22,198	19,064	17,499	-14.1	-8.2
HS diploma to some college	27,520	26,069	24,021	-5.3	-7.9
BA/BS or higher degree	40,398	42,587	42,007	5.4	-1.4

Note: We set topcoding of the three components of earnings (wages and salaries, self-employment earnings, and farm self-employment earnings) in 1989 and 1995 at current values comparable to the $50,000 topcodes for each component used by the Census Bureau in the 1979 CPS file. See Appendix I for more details.

Source: Calculated by the authors using data from the March 1979, 1990, and 1996 Current Population Survey files.

fixed. In the 1980's, this specialization increased, as low-education production sector jobs shifted to rural areas (and abroad) and high-education jobs became increasingly concentrated in urban areas. The 1980's saw a strong increase in urban production sector wages for the highly educated and a migration flow of young, highly educated workers to urban areas. Rural areas were not participating in the New Economy of the time.

Our analysis of trends in the 1990's suggests that the tendency for high-education activities to concentrate in urban areas did not continue into this decade,

TABLE 8.11. Urban and rural earnings by industry and education as percents of national average earnings[a]

	Ages 18-64		Ages 18-34	
	Urban	Rural	Urban	Rural
1995				
Total	104	81	103	85
Consumer services sector	98	80	97	81
No HS diploma	62	60	66	59
HS diploma to some college	85	74	87	78
BA/BS or higher degree	135	107	132	106
Production sector	114	84	113	90
No HS diploma	61	65	67	69
HS diploma to some college	96	80	95	85
BA/BS or higher degree	163	131	162	151
1989				
Total	105	80	105	80
Consumer services sector	98	78	98	79
No HS diploma	67	58	68	57
HS diploma to some college	88	71	91	76
BA/BS or higher degree	132	111	128	101
Production sector	115	83	114	83
No HS diploma	70	63	71	66
HS diploma to some college	99	81	99	82
BA/BS or higher degree	164	128	158	119
1978				
Total	105	88	103	92
Consumer services sector	100	86	99	91
No HS diploma	80	69	80	73
HS diploma to some college	91	80	91	86
BA/BS or higher degree	133	118	122	115
Production sector	112	91	109	93
No HS diploma	85	72	83	74
HS diploma to some college	102	89	103	90
BA/BS or higher degree	165	144	147	136

Source: Calculated by the authors using data from the March 1979, 1990, and 1996 Current Population Survey files.

Notes: We set topcoding of the three components of earnings (wages and salaries, self-employment earnings, and farm self-employment earnings) in 1989 and 1995 at current values comparable to the $50,000 topcodes for each component used by the Census Bureau in the 1979 CPS file. See Appendix I for more details. Urban-rural designations of areas vary between each year analyzed, with more of the nation designated as metropolitan each year.

[a]Within each age group, average earnings of full-time, full-year workers in each residence/industry/education category were divided by national average earnings of all full-time, full-year workers in the age group and multiplied by 100.

although there is no clear, consistent evidence of decentralization. The basic differences in the industrial structures of the rural and urban economies remained unchanged between 1990 and 1996, at least as measured by indexes of dissimilarity. The analysis of changes in the educational requirements of jobs suggests that jobs for the college educated have continued to rise more rapidly in urban areas, although the differences are attributable to the slower growth nationally of the types of high-education jobs located in rural areas rather than a shift of high-education jobs from rural to urban areas, such as occurred in the 1980's. Rural high-education jobs are more often in manufacturing than are urban jobs, and manufacturing added relatively few of these jobs in the 1990–96 period, at least compared with producer services industries. Indications that production sector high-education jobs are becoming more available in rural areas include the net migration of working-age college-educated population into rural areas and a rise in the relative earnings of college graduates in rural areas, particularly for young adults in the production sector.

Also gone in the 1990's is the tendency for low-education production sector jobs to shift to rural areas. While continuing to decline in rural areas, the proportion of jobs typically filled by people without a high school diploma actually increased in urban areas between 1989 and 1995. Since the number of urban working-age people without a high school diploma declined, a substantial proportion of these low-education jobs are being filled by people with higher levels of education. One reason that the earnings of workers without high school diplomas have fallen so sharply in urban areas may be that these workers are left with only the lowest paying of these jobs. On the other hand, there may have been skill upgrading within these jobs, a change not reflected in our method of measuring changes in skill needs. In contrast to the urban experience, rural areas have seen a growth in middle education jobs relative to other jobs.

Earnings inequality between college graduates and other earners has grown considerably during the past 20 years. During the 1980's this growth in inequality was primarily an urban phenomenon, but it has spread to rural areas in the 1990's, with a marked rise in the earnings of young rural college graduates. The precise reasons for the increasing inequality are not well understood but appear to reflect a combination of technological change, changes in trade, and other factors such as the decline in union power (Johnson 1997; Topel 1997; Fortin and Lemieux 1997).

Increasing job opportunities and higher earnings for the most educated and declining opportunities and earnings for the less educated raise two different sets of concerns for rural regions: (1) are rural educational systems enabling rural youth to take advantage of new opportunities in the labor market, wherever they may end up living, and (2) can rural regions adapt to the changing economy and attract higher-level jobs? Previous chapters in this book show that rural areas generally prepare students well up through the high school level—although the South, despite considerable gains, remains somewhat behind. But given the declining earnings opportunities for high school dropouts, current rural dropout rates, while at an historic low, remain higher than desired.

The high premium currently earned by workers with a college degree places rural youth (as well as the rural population in general) at a significant disadvantage. Rural schools are not organized around getting students into college, and with relatively few local four-year colleges, rural students have fewer opportunities than urban students to attend local colleges while living at home. The expansion of local community colleges has been especially beneficial for rural students and has increased the likelihood that rural youth will go on to college—at least in areas where these colleges exist (Chapter 4). The balanced budget agreement of 1997 magnifies this effect by providing for scholarships as large as $1,500 for the first two years of college. But at present, it is clear that an associate's degree remains far less marketable than a bachelor's degree, so the ability of community colleges to foster and prepare students for further education is critical.

While the college-educated population has grown more rapidly than any other rural education group in recent decades, the proportion of college educated in the rural population remains extremely low. Rural areas have not kept or attracted back their college graduates. In the 1980's, there were clearly more urban opportunities for young adults with a college education, and moving to a rural area often meant a considerable financial sacrifice. In the 1990's, there are indications that rural demand for workers with college degrees has picked up and that there may be shortages in areas that are remote or less attractive places to live. Not only have earnings, at least among young adults, risen for workers with a college degree, but there has been a small net outflow of college educated from urban to rural areas. Moreover, many manufacturers are reporting problems in attracting managers and professionals to their plants, particularly in areas of low population density such as the Great Plains. Among the factors that probably make it difficult for some areas to attract professionals and managers are low-quality schools, harsh climates, or the lack of urban amenities. In addition, with the increasing frequency of dual-career households, moving to a rural area that has fewer suitable jobs within commuting distance can be quite difficult for this highly educated group. And it may not be just a question of a single move. In urban areas, one can frequently advance by moving to another organization in the same area. In rural areas, advancement—whether for school principals, mechanical engineers, or doctors—most often means moving to another area, and moves are difficult on families in general and dual-career households in particular.

The situation for those with less education is somewhat more difficult to evaluate. The quality of available labor is a central issue for both rural and urban manufacturers and for employers in general. One type of solution is to organize production and service activities around low-skill, low-wage labor. This appears to be an important part of recent changes in the urban economy. At the other extreme is the organization of those activities around skilled labor with new technologies. Rural economic opportunities for workers with less than a college degree appear to have improved marginally in the early 1990's, but it is not clear whether rural employers are going to follow a low-skill or high-skill route. In the long run, it would appear that areas, whether rural or urban, that are best able to raise the quality of local labor to handle new technologies will have the best chance for sustainable economic growth—and the best chance for improving the economic opportunities for those without a college degree. Solving the problem of labor quality clearly goes beyond getting more youth to finish high school and to take further courses. The solution involves developing the ability of local educational institutions—high schools, community colleges, training institutes, and others—to work with local employers and potential employers to meet their needs and to improve the abilities and earnings of the local workforce.

APPENDIX TABLE 8.1. Percent distribution of urban and rural jobs by educational requirements within industries, 1995

	No HS diploma	HS diploma	Some college	BA/BS degree	Higher degree	Total
Urban	11.1	33.4	30.3	16.2	9.0	100.0
Production sector						
Agriculture, forestry, and fishing	30.9	39.0	19.9	8.2	1.9	100.0
Mining	12.8	32.5	24.5	22.8	7.5	100.0
Total manufacturing	15.3	38.9	26.7	14.2	4.9	100.0
Routine	21.5	44.5	22.9	8.8	2.3	100.0
Complex	9.2	33.3	30.4	19.5	7.5	100.0
Business services	7.2	27.0	32.5	22.8	10.5	100.0
Total	11.7	32.9	29.3	18.4	7.6	100.0
Consumer services sector						
Distribution	9.7	37.9	33.9	15.0	3.5	100.0
Retail and personal	15.4	41.0	30.4	10.8	2.5	100.0
Health, education, and professional	4.7	20.8	29.0	21.7	23.9	100.0
Government	3.0	25.7	38.2	21.9	11.2	100.0
Construction	18.4	43.1	28.0	8.4	2.1	100.0
Total	10.7	33.6	30.8	15.2	9.6	100.0
Rural	14.9	37.8	28.4	12.5	6.4	100.0
Production sector						
Agriculture, forestry, and fishing	26.0	40.9	21.8	9.6	1.8	100.0
Mining	18.6	43.9	23.6	10.9	3.0	100.0
Total manufacturing	22.4	46.4	22.4	6.8	2.0	100.0
Routine	25.7	47.7	20.0	5.2	1.3	100.0
Complex	14.0	43.1	28.5	10.8	3.6	100.0
Business services	9.5	31.5	33.1	18.9	7.0	100.0
Total	19.6	41.8	25.0	10.4	3.2	100.0
Consumer services sector						
Distribution	13.0	42.3	31.4	40.9	2.4	100.0
Retail and personal	15.8	41.4	30.2	10.1	2.4	100.0
Health, education, and professional	5.8	22.3	29.2	21.3	21.4	100.0
Government	4.0	27.2	38.5	20.6	9.8	100.0
Construction	20.5	45.3	26.5	6.3	1.4	100.0
Total	12.3	35.6	30.3	13.6	8.1	100.0

Source: Calculated by the authors using data from the March 1996 Current Population Survey.

APPENDIX TABLE **8.2.** Percent change in industry employment by education requirements of jobs, 1990-96

	No HS diploma	HS diploma	Some college	BA/BS degree	Higher degree	Total
National	6.1	4.9	6.0	9.0	10.9	6.5
Production sector	2.7	0.4	2.2	10.2	10.8	3.4
Agriculture, forestry, and fishing	-1.1	-2.7	-3.3	-8.9	-14.9	-3.2
Mining	-27.2	-26.3	-25.3	-11.9	-17.1	-23.7
Total manufacturing	-2.0	-3.7	-4.7	2.5	6.6	-2.5
Routine	-0.8	-2.1	-4.1	-2.5	-0.4	-2.2
Complex	-5.2	-6.2	-5.2	5.3	9.3	-2.9
Business services	22.6	10.4	10.6	17.3	14.1	13.2
Consumer services sector	8.3	7.2	7.8	8.3	10.9	8.0
Distribution	-0.2	-2	-2.8	1.1	4	- 1.5
Retail and personal	13.9	12.2	14.2	15.5	16	13.5
Health, education, and professional	6.1	9.3	9	6.8	10.3	8.7
Government	-5.2	-1.7	1.7	9.9	18.8	3.8
Construction	2.5	4.6	6.3	4.2	1.3	4.6
Urban	6.8	4.9	5.9	9.0	11.3	6.6
Production sector	3.4	0	2.2	10.7	11.6	3.7
Agriculture, forestry, and fishing	-1.4	-7.8	-9.9	-18.6	-19.9	-7.7
Mining	-29.5	-33	-32.5	-17.1	-21.7	-28.6
Total manufacturing	-3.0	-5.1	-5.5	3.0	7.1	-3.3
Routine	-1.5	-3.6	-5.7	-2.6	-0.5	-3.5
Complex	-6.3	-7.1	-5.4	5.6	9.6	-3.1
Business services	23.3	10.1	10.5	17.4	14.9	13.2
Consumer services sector	8.6	7.3	7.6	8.1	11.2	8.0
Distribution	- 1.9	-3.1	-3.5	0.6	3.4	-2.4
Retail and personal	14.8	12.8	14.4	15.1	14.4	13.9
Health, education, and professional	6.4	9.4	9.0	7.0	11.1	9.0
Government	-8.0	-2.3	1.2	8.9	17.5	3.2
Construction	3.3	5.1	6.5	4.3	1.4	5.0
Rural	4.1	4.8	6.7	8.7	8.2	5.9
Production sector	0.9	1.6	2.5	6.6	3.1	2.2
Agriculture, forestry, and fishing	-0.9	1.4	2.0	-1.1	-10.4	0.4
Mining	-25.5	-20.3	-15.9	1.5	-2.5	-18
Total manufacturing	0.5	0.4	-1.3	-0.4	2.8	0
Routine	0.7	1.4	0.4	-2.2	-0.2	0.8
Complex	-0.5	-2.3	-4.4	1.9	5.6	-2.0
Business services	18.7	12.2	11.8	16.4	6.1	13.0
Consumer services sector	7.0	7.0	8.7	9.6	9.4	8.1
Distribution	6.8	3.7	1.4	5.0	9.6	3.6
Retail and personal	10.5	9.7	13.4	17.4	23.5	12.0
Health, education, and professional	5.0	8.6	9.0	5.5	6.1	7.3
Government	6.1	0.9	3.9	15.1	26.1	7.1
Construction	-0.2	3.0	5.6	3.8	0.7	3.0

Source: Calculated by the authors using data from the 1990 Census of Population public use microdata file and the March 1996 Current Population Survey.

APPENDIX I: METHODS

Analysis of trends requires that the same information be collected for the same areas over the time period being analyzed, preferably with the same survey instrument. Evidence of changes in education required by jobs and worker education levels in metro and nonmetro America remains piecemeal, at least partly because data collected on residence, occupations, and industries varied during 1970–96.

The two primary sources of education data, the decennial Census and annual Current Population Survey (CPS), changed both metro-nonmetro designations and occupation and industry classifications during the 1970's, 1980's, and 1990's. And new educational attainment categories were adopted in the 1990's. Because of this lack of a consistent time series, we used several combinations of Census and CPS data to investigate metro-nonmetro differences in educational requirements of jobs and the supply of education in the working-age population.

The levels of educational attainment we used in our previous analysis of the 1970's and 1980's were measured in years of schooling completed: less than high school (0–11 years), high school graduate (12 years), some college (13–15 years), college graduate (16 years), and 5 or more years of college (17 or more years) (McGranahan and Ghelfi 1991). The levels of educational attainment in the 1990's analysis are measured in degrees attained: did not obtain a high school diploma or GED (No HS diploma), obtained a high school diploma or GED (HS diploma), attended some college, including obtaining an associate's degree, but did not get a bachelor's degree (Some college), obtained a bachelor's degree (BA/BS), obtained a master's or more advanced degree (Higher degree).

ADJUSTMENTS FOR DATA DIFFERENCES

We made adjustments for some of the differences among the Census and CPS files. Unclassified cases on the CPS files were allocated to metro and nonmetro areas, and adjustments were made for differing metro-nonmetro designations on the 1990 Census and 1996 CPS files.

Unclassified Cases on the CPS File

The public use data file from the 1996 March CPS identifies most persons by their metro or nonmetro residence. However, a small proportion of the population in sampling units in three states was left unclassified for confidentiality reasons. We assigned the unclassified cases to metro and nonmetro areas in proportion to Census Bureau published numbers of persons in each unit. Our weighting procedure averages the characteristics of the unclassified cases and adds them disproportionately to nonmetro areas, reflecting the fact that the populations in these units are disproportionately nonmetro. The higher educational attainment and occupational status of metro residents in general leads us to believe the average characteristics of the unclassified groups are an overestimate of the status of the nonmetro portion of that group. However, the unclassified cases accounted for only 0.9 percent of nonmetro persons 18 to 64 years old and 0.1 percent of metro persons. We feel that at those levels, the slight upward bias in the characteristics of the unclassifieds does not significantly bias our results.

Differences in Metro-Nonmetro Designations

The 1990 Census and the March 1996 CPS files differ slightly in their metro-nonmetro designations. The 1990 Census public use file uses a metro-nonmetro definition that does not consider 1990 intercounty commuting in determining whether a county is part of a metropolitan area. The metro-nonmetro designation used in the 1996 CPS files uses the 1990 commuting patterns. A few counties considered metro by the 1990 Census lost their metro status when current commuting was considered. A larger number of counties considered nonmetro by the 1990 Census were reclassified to metro by commuting patterns. If the metro-nonmetro designation on the 1990 Census file had been based on current commuting, the nonmetro population in 1990 would have been 8.1 percent smaller.

Measures of growth in jobs and labor supply by education level would overestimate metro growth and underestimate nonmetro growth if we did not adjust for this difference in designations. The specific adjustments we made are explained in the education required and education supply sections below.

The Small CPS Sample

We would like to have had the opportunity to strengthen the 1996 CPS estimates by averaging its results with results from another year, as we did with the 1987 and 1988 CPS's in our earlier analysis (McGranahan and Ghelfi 1991), but the Census Bureau moved to the 1990 metro-nonmetro designation of sampling areas during 1995, so that year does not have a reliable metro-nonmetro breakdown, and the March 1997 file was not available at the time of this analysis. With both a smaller CPS sample and a smaller nonmetro population in 1996, the estimates we present should be viewed as indicators of direction and magnitude of change, but not as precise indicators.

ESTIMATES OF EDUCATION REQUIREMENTS

Education required is the education level that is desired to perform the work involved in a job. Our 1989–95 estimates of education need are based, like our 1970–79 and 1980–87/88 estimates were, on the education levels of full-time, full-year workers in each of 18 industry groups. Within each industry group, workers were further disaggregated into 25 occupational groups (see Appendix II for definitions of occupation and industry categories). Not all industries employed workers in all occupations, so the number of job types totaled 443. The one difference between our 1989–95 analysis and our previous decades' analyses is that we used the industry and occupation of the longest held job in the previous year rather than the industry and occupation of the current job.

Data Adjustments

We calculated education required within each industry-occupation job type based on the distribution of full-time, full-year workers in 1989 by education level from the 1990 Census. This calculation of educational need assumed, in effect, that supply and demand were in equilibrium across job types at the time of the Census: that is, that the Census distributions reflected the distribution across job types of education desired by both employers and employees (the distribution is adequate for the work performed while the skills of the workers are fully used). We used the educational distribution of full-time, full-year workers to reflect as accurately as possible the education required by each job type.

Using full-time, full-year workers for the entire analysis, however, would have biased the distribution of employment in favor of industries that employ higher proportions of those workers. Retail industries and other employers of high proportions of part-time workers would have been underrepresented.

To incorporate the educational requirements of jobs reflected in the educational levels of full-time, full-year workers and also to analyze the distribution of all employed workers, we used the proportion of full-time, full-year workers at each education level within a job type as "standard educational requirements" and applied those proportions to all workers employed in that job type. We applied the 1989 "standard" to national, metro, and nonmetro workers in 1989 (Census data) and 1995 (March CPS data).

Before applying the "standard" education proportions, we adjusted for the difference in metro-nonmetro classification between the 1990 Census and the 1996 CPS's by subtracting 8.1 percent (2 million) of total nonmetro jobs in 1989 and adding them to metro jobs. We assumed that the industrial and occupational distribution of these jobs was intermediate between the metro and nonmetro distributions. The number of jobs reassigned from nonmetro to metro in each industry/occupation group was determined as follows:

ADJUSTMENT = $2{,}031{,}420 * (((\text{NOCCIND}/\text{NTOT}) + (\text{MOCCIND}/\text{MTOT}))/2)$

Where:
NOCCIND = nonmetro number in industry/occupation group
MOCCIND = metro number in industry/occupation group
NTOT = total nonmetro jobs before adjustment
MTOT = total metro jobs before adjustment

The Education Requirements Estimation Procedure

Here is a simplified example of our education requirements estimation process. In 1989, there were 320 (for example, not in reality) full-time, full-year social workers throughout the United States who were distributed by education as follows:

Item	Total	No HS diploma	HS diploma	Some college	BA/BS	Higher degree
Full-time, full-year social workers	320	18	46	80	111	65
"Standard" proportion in each education category	1.00	.06	.14	.25	.35	.20

Education required of all social workers nationally and in metro and nonmetro areas in 1989 and 1995 was then estimated by multiplying the total number of social workers in those areas and years by the "standard" proportions (estimated numbers are in bold type):

Item	Total	No HS diploma	HS diploma	Some college	BA/BS	Higher degree
1989						
Total	410	**25**	**57**	**102**	**144**	**82**
Metro*	309	**19**	**43**	**77**	**108**	**62**
Nonmetro*	101	**6**	**14**	**25**	**36**	**20**
1995						
Total	514	**31**	**72**	**128**	**180**	**103**
Metro	400	**24**	**56**	**100**	**140**	**80**
Nonmetro	114	**7**	**16**	**28**	**40**	**23**

*Adjusted to reflect CPS metro-nonmetro designation.

In the full-scale analysis, the educational distribution of workers in each of the industry/occupation job types in each year was computed. Then workers in each educational category were summed across all job types to total requirements for each level of education. Education required in production and consumer services industries was also estimated for each year by summing the number of workers at each education level across the occupation/industry categories in production and consumer services industries (see Appendix II for definitions of industries categorized as production and consumer services).

This method assumes that the same education required by occupations and industries in 1989 was required in 1995. Educational upgrading of jobs is not taken into account. Retirees have typically had less education than their replacements. Also, technological change in manufacturing processes requires a more highly educated labor force. Thus, our estimates of change in requirements for more highly educated workers undoubtedly underestimate actual increases in need (as we have defined it). We assume that this change has not occurred unevenly enough to seriously bias our results.

JOB SHIFT-SHARE REDISTRIBUTION

Another measure of change in education requirements that we calculated is job redistribution. This measure is a shift-share type indicator based on the difference between actual growth in nonmetro jobs by education level and the growth that would be expected had nonmetro jobs in each industry/occupation category grown at the same rate as metro jobs.

For each decade, redistribution of jobs by education level between metro and nonmetro areas was estimated in a five-step process:

1. For each education level within each industry/occupation category, the number of nonmetro workers in 1990 was subtracted from the number of nonmetro workers in 1996 to obtain actual change.

2. For each education level within each industry/occupation category, the number of nonmetro workers in 1990 was multiplied by the percent the cell changed in metro areas from 1990 to 1996, with the goal of obtaining expected change.

3. Actual change, expected change, and total nonmetro workers in 1990 at each education level were then summed to overall, production, and consumer services sector totals.

4. Actual and expected change totals were divided by 1990 workers to obtain actual and expected percent change at each education level.

5. Expected percent change was subtracted from actual percent change to obtain the percent of production sector, consumer services sector, and all jobs at each education level that were redistributed to or from metro areas in each decade.

Table 8.5. shows the results of this analysis. The results for 1980–88 shown in that table are taken from our earlier analysis of the 1970's and 1980's.

ESTIMATES OF EDUCATION SUPPLY

Education supply is the number of people at each education level who are available for work. To estimate the supply of education, we relied on four population subgroups. We looked at 18- to 64-year-olds and 25- to 34-year-olds, the total population in each age group and those in the labor force. The total population in either of these age groups is clearly an overestimate of the number of people available for work. Some people are not available for work due to early retirement, caring for children, a mental or physical disability, or other reasons. Those in the labor force underestimate the number available for work. Some of those who are neither working nor looking for work (not in the labor force) may be available for work but are not looking because they feel there are no jobs available. Others might enter the labor force if family circumstances changed (such as divorce or the youngest child entering school), if a job with the "right" hours or wage rate became available, or for some other reason. We presented education levels for both populations as upper- and lower-bound estimates of labor supply. Again we adjusted the 1990 data to account for differences in the 1990 Census and 1996 CPS metro-nonmetro designations.

RETURNS TO EDUCATION

We looked at returns to education as an indicator of the intersection of supply and demand for education. The average annual earnings by education level for 18- to 64-year-olds and for 18- to 34-year-olds working full-time, full-year were calculated from March 1979, 1990, and 1996 CPS files. Earnings in all three years were adjusted to 1995 dollars using the chained price deflator for Personal Consumption Expenditures (PCE). Because the Census Bureau raised its topcoding cutoffs faster than inflation between each year we analyzed, we set lower topcodes in 1989 and 1995 (the years for which respondents to the March 1990 and 1996 CPS's were asked to report earnings) for each of the three components of earnings (wages and salaries, nonfarm self-employment earnings, and farm self-employment earnings). The level at which the Census Bureau topped off 1978 earnings was $50,000 for each of the three components. Using the chained price deflator for Personal Consumption Expenditures, we calculated and applied a topcode of $91,000 in 1989 and a topcode of $111,000 in 1995 to keep earnings change from reflecting the simple recording of higher earnings at the top end of the distribution rather than real earnings growth. The earnings changes we show in Table 8.10 are then lower than what would be found if we had used the original 1990 and 1996 CPS topcodes.

The three CPS's are based on different designations of metro and nonmetro areas. In analyzing earnings, we could and did reweight unidentified cases to apportion them between metro and nonmetro areas as we had done for education supply and demand, but we did not have a means of adjusting for the different area designations. Nonmetro areas lost counties to metro designation between each of the years we analyzed. The counties that nonmetro areas lose generally are those with cities that grow to meet the metro (50,000 or more residents) standard and those that increase their commuting to metro jobs. On average, earnings in the lost counties are higher than in the remaining nonmetro counties, but lower than established metro counties, thereby dampening estimates of earnings change for both groups.

COMPARISONS INVOLVING CENSUS AND CPS DATA

Much of our analysis relied on comparisons between Census data and CPS data. CPS data are benchmarked to the previous Census, but some of the changes we found over a decade may reflect differences in CPS and Census data collection methods rather than actual change. Where possible, we tried to check our results against other data. For instance, the Bureau of Economic Analysis has industry employment data that, like our data, show an increasing rural-urban division of labor in the 1980's.

APPENDIX II: INDUSTRY AND OCCUPATION DEFINITIONS

INDUSTRY CATEGORIES USED IN EDUCATION DEMAND ANALYSIS

Production Sector Industries

Agriculture, forestry, and fishing
Mining
Textile and apparel manufacturing
Other routine manufacturing usually done by small firms:
> lumber, wood, and furniture products; cement, concrete, gypsum, plaster, and clay products; screw machine products; miscellaneous fabricated metal products; mobile dwellings and campers; cycles and miscellaneous transportation equipment; watches, clocks, and clockwork-operated devices; miscellaneous durable manufacturing industries; meat and dairy products; fruit, vegetable, and seafood canning and preserving; confectionery and related products; miscellaneous plastic products; and leather and leather products

Other routine manufacturing usually done by large firms:
> glass and glass products; blast furnaces; steel works; metal rolling and finishing mills; other primary iron and steel industries; metal stamping; farm machinery and equipment; electrical household appliances; motor vehicles and equipment; railroad locomotives and equipment; bakery products; beverages; tobacco products; paper and allied products; and rubber products

Complex manufacturing usually done by small firms:
> nonmetallic mineral and stone products; fabricated structural metal products; nonelectrical metal-working machinery; electrical machines, equipment, and supplies; optical and health service supplies; printing, publishing, and allied industries except newspapers; soaps and cosmetics; and varnishes, paints, and related products

Complex manufacturing usually done by large firms:
> engines and turbines; construction and material-handling machines; office and accounting machines; electronic computing equipment; radio, television, and communication equipment; aircraft and parts; scientific and controlling equipment; photographic equipment and supplies; ordnance; grain-mill products; industrial chemicals; plastics, synthetics, and resins; drugs and medicines; agricultural chemicals; miscellaneous chemicals; petroleum refining; and miscellaneous petroleum and coal products

Higher-technology producer services:
banking; security, commodity brokerage, and investment companies; insurance firms; real estate and combined real estate-insurance-law offices; advertising firms; commercial research, development, and testing laboratories; business management and consulting services; computer programming services; legal services; engineering and architectural services; accounting, auditing, and bookkeeping services; and miscellaneous professional and related services

Lower-technology producer services:
custodial and other services to residences and other buildings; employment and temporary help agencies; detective and protective services; electrical repair shops; miscellaneous repair services; and hotels and motels

Consumer Services Sector Industries

Information services and air transportation:
telephone, telegraph, and miscellaneous communication services; and air transportation

Transportation, except air:
postal service; railroads; railway express services; street railways; taxicab services; trucking, warehousing, and storage services; water transportation; pipelines, except natural gas; and services incidental to transportation

Public utilities:
electric, gas, steam supply, water supply, sanitary service, and other utilities

Wholesale trade

Retail trade

Professional consumer services:
newspaper publishing and printing; radio and television broadcasting; financial credit agencies; offices of physicians, dentists, chiropractors, and other health practitioners; other health services; elementary and secondary schools; colleges and universities; libraries; other educational services; museums, art galleries, and zoos; religious organizations; welfare services; residential welfare facilities; and nonprofit membership organizations

Personal consumer services:
horticultural services; private household services; lodging places, except hotels and motels; laundering, cleaning, and other garment services; beauty and barbershops; shoe repair and dressmaking shops; entertainment and recreation services; and convalescent institutions

Government

Construction

Occupational Categories Used in Education Demand Analysis

Executives, administrators, and managers:
legislators, chief executives, administrators, and officials in public administration; financial, personnel, labor relations, purchasing, marketing, advertising, public relations, medical, health, property, and real estate managers; funeral directors; education and related field administrators; protective service administrators; and postmasters and mail superintendents

Management-related workers:
accountants, auditors, underwriters, financial officers, management analysts, purchasing agents, buyers, business agents, promotion agents, inspectors, and compliance officers

High-education professionals:
architects, physicians, dentists, veterinarians, college and university teachers, lawyers, and judges

Medium-education professionals:
computer systems analysts, operations analysts, systems analysts, actuaries, statisticians, mathematical scientists, natural scientists, optometrists, podiatrists, social scientists, and urban planners

Lower-education professionals:
engineers, registered nurses, pharmacists, dieticians, therapists, physicians' assistants, teachers other than college and university, educational and vocational counselors, librarians, archivists, curators, social workers, clergy, religious workers, and recreation workers

Artistic professionals:
authors, technical writers, designers, musicians, composers, actors, directors, painters, sculptors, craft-artists, artist printmakers, photographers, dancers, editors, reporters, announcers, athletes, and public relations specialists

Technicians and technologists:
technicians and technologists working in health, engineering, drafting, surveying, mapping, and sciences; airplane pilots and navigators; air traffic controllers; broadcast equipment operators; computer programmers; and legal assistants

Sales supervisors and proprietors

Sales representatives:
sales representatives in finance, business services, mining, manufacturing, and wholesale trade

Sales workers:
sales workers in retail and personal services including sales counter clerks, cashiers, and door-to-door sellers; demonstrators; promoters; sales models; and auctioneers

Administrative support supervisors:
supervisors of computer equipment, financial records, communications equipment, and distribution workers

Administrative support workers:
  computer equipment operators; financial records processing clerks and
  machine operators; adjusters; and investigators
Clerical workers:
  secretaries, stenographers, typists, information clerks other than financial
  records–processing clerks, office machine operators, communications equipment operators, mail clerks and carriers, messengers, dispatchers, shipping
  and receiving clerks, stock and inventory clerks, meter readers, weighers,
  samplers, measurers, checkers, expediters, general office clerks, bank tellers,
  proofreaders, data-entry keyers, statistical clerks, and teachers' aides
Service supervisors
High-education service workers:
  dental assistants; health aides; therapy assistants; nursing aides; orderlies; bar-
  bers; hairdressers; cosmetologists; welfare service aides; and publicly
  employed firefighters, police officers, marshals, constables, detectives, sher-
  iffs, bailiffs, and correctional institution officers
Low-education service workers:
  private household workers; privately employed guards, police, and detectives;
  crossing guards; food and beverage preparation and serving workers; build-
  ing-cleaning workers; elevator operators; pest control workers; amusement
  and recreation facility attendants; ushers; guides; public transportation attendants; baggage porters; bellhops; and child care workers
Farmers and farm managers and fishing vessel captains and officers
Labor supervisors
Laborers:
  farmworkers; groundskeepers; gardeners; animal caretakers; agricultural
  product graders, sorters, and inspectors; horticultural nursery workers;
  forestry workers; timber-cutting and logging workers; fishers; hunters; trap-
  pers; construction laborers; helpers in mechanic, repair, construction, and
  extractive industries; production helpers; garbage collectors; stevedores; stock
  handlers and baggers; machine feeders and offbearers; garage and service sta-
  tion attendants; vehicle washers; equipment cleaners; and hand packers and
  packagers
Precision production, machine operator, and hand fabricator, grader, checker, and
packer supervisors
Precision production workers:
  mechanics and machinery repairers; brickmasons, stonemasons, carpenters,
  electricians, painters, plasterers, plumbers, roofers, glaziers, and other construction tradespersons; drillers, explosives workers, and other mining occupations; tool and die makers, machinists, metal engravers, and other precision
  metal-working occupations; cabinetmakers, furniture and wood finishers, and
  other precision woodworkers; dressmakers, tailors, shoe repairers, upholster-
  ers, and other precision textile and apparel workers; bookbinders; dental laboratory technicians; optical goods workers; medical appliance technicians;

butchers and meat cutters; bakers; precision inspectors, testers, and graders; water and sewage plant operators; power plant operators; and stationary engineers

Machine operators:

metal- and plastic-working machine operators; woodworking machine operators; printing machine operators; textile and apparel machine operators; gluing, packaging, extruding, molding, separating, compressing, roasting, washing, folding, crushing, slicing, and cutting machine operators; motion picture protectionists; and photographic process machine operators

Hand fabricators, graders, checkers, and packers:

welders; cutters; solderers; blazers; hand cutters, trimmers, molders, casters, painters, engravers, printers, grinders, and polishers; and production inspectors, checkers, examiners, testers, samplers, weighers, graders, and sorters

Transportation and material mover supervisors

Transportation and material moving workers:

truck, bus, and taxicab drivers; parking lot attendants; rail and water transportation workers; longshore equipment operators; hoist, winch, and crane operators; excavating and loading equipment operators; grader, dozer, and scraper operators; and industrial truck and tractor equipment operators

NOTES

1 Unless otherwise noted, information on changes in the 1980's are from this report chapter.

2 The idea of two economic sectors is neater than the reality. Several industries, such as banking and transportation, serve both producers and residential consumers. Because of their central role in the internationalization of markets, we assigned banking, legal, accounting, and related services to the production sector. Industries involved with distribution—wholesale, transportation, communication, and utilities—were assigned to the consumer services sector because we felt that the territorial division of labor of these distributive industries depends at least as much on the location of consumers as on the location of other industries. Finally, some consumer services act as part of a local economic base—i.e., bring in outside money—when they serve tourists or conventioneers. See Appendix II for the classification of industries.

3 Our method is more fully detailed in Appendix I.

4 The 1989-95 comparisons used in this study must be seen as more tentative than comparisons for earlier decades. The Current Population Survey (CPS) has undergone considerable change during the 1990's. Most notable for the current analysis is that while the 1996 sampling frame was based on the 1990 Population Census, the frame was adjusted to take into account estimates of Census undercounting, an extra step not made in previous decades. This has tended to boost estimates of minority populations—and occupants of low-education jobs. The CPS overall 1990 national unemployment rate estimates rose by only .1 percentage points with the new estimates, suggesting that the net effect may not have been large (McIntire, 1996).

5 Some of the reduction in midlevel jobs in manufacturing may have been the result of outsourcing. However, the same pattern appeared in producer services, which would have been the industry group doing much of outsourced work.

6 Data from the 1996 Economic Research Service Rural Manufacturing Survey, which covered nearly 4,000 plants in rural and urban areas, show that urban plants tend to have lower proportions of production workers with high school diplomas than rural plants. This is true in the South as well as the country as a whole.

7 We have used the 25–64 population rather than the 18–64 population as much of migration in the late teens and early 20's is associated with college attendance.

8 The publicly released Current Population Survey (CPS) data sets have top-coded annual earnings. Prior to the March 1996 file (for 1995 earnings), this meant the imposition of an upper bound on earnings, which was raised periodically as national earnings levels rose. In the March 1996 file, when earnings exceeded the top code, a representative earnings amount was assigned to the earner based on the earnings of similar earners. To ensure that our earnings trends would represent real changes in the distribution of earners among industry and education categories rather than changes in the top-coding procedure, the earnings in Table 8.10 are calculated with top codes for 1989 and 1995 that are equal in real terms to the top code in the 1978 data. Very low percentages of earners in the two lower education categories had high enough earnings to be top coded in any year, so their earnings are virtually unaffected. The proportion of college graduate earners (ages 18–64) whose earnings we top coded rose from 1.7 percent in 1979 to 4.7 percent in 1995.

Estimated earnings based on the original data show that our top coding substantially reduced earnings in the college graduate group in 1995, even though relatively few cases are involved.

9 The size of this gain is suspiciously large. CPS weekly earnings data files, based on all monthly surveys and averaged for the year, provide a larger number of cases. A brief examination of these data for 1990–95 found changes largely consistent with the findings presented here, except for a small rise in earnings among young urban college graduates (our data show a decline). The production and consumer services sectors were not split out in that analysis, however.

REFERENCES

Beyers, William B. and David P. Lindahl. 1996. "Lone Eagles and High Fliers in Rural Producer Services." *Rural Development Perspectives* 11, no. 3 (June):2–10.

Broadway, Michael J. 1994. "Hogtowns and Rural Development." *Rural Development Perspectives* 9, no. 2 (February):40–46.

Burtless, Gary (ed.). 1990. *A Future of Lousy Jobs? The Changing Structure of U.S. Wages*. Washington, DC: The Brookings Institution.

Cooper, Helene. 1997. "Nogales, Ariz., Throws a Post NAFTA Party, but Locals Miss Out." *Wall Street Journal*, March 21, p. 1.

Dertouzos, Michael L., Richard K. Lester, and Robert M. Solow. 1989. *Made in America: Regaining the Productive Edge*. Cambridge, MA: MIT Press.

Fortin, Nicole M. and Thomas Lemieux. 1997. "Institutional Changes and Rising Wage Inequality: Is There a Link?" *Journal of Economic Perspectives* 11, no. 2 (Spring):75–96.

Gale, H. Frederick. 1997. *Is There a Rural-Urban Technology Gap?* U.S. Department of Agriculture, Economic Research Service, Agriculture Issue Brief No. 736-01, July.

Johnson, George E. 1997. "Changes in Earnings Inequality: The Role of Demand Shifts." *Journal of Economic Perspectives*, 11, no. 2 (Spring):41–54.

Lee, Chinkook and Kenneth Hanson. 1997. "The Factor Content of U.S. Trade: An Explanation for the Widening Wage Gap?" Paper presented at the Western Agricultural Economics Association Meetings, July 13–17, at Sacramento, CA.

Levy, Frank. 1987. Dollars and Dreams: *The Changing American Income Distribution*. New York: Russell Sage.

McGranahan, David A. 1988. "Rural Workers in the National Economy." In *Rural Development in the 1980's: Prospects for the Future*, edited by David B. Brown, J. Norman Reid, Herman Bluestone, David A. McGranahan, and Sara M. Mazie. RDRR-69, U.S. Department of Agriculture, Economic Research Service, September.

McGranahan, David A. and Linda M. Ghelfi. 1991. "The Education Crisis and Rural Stagnation in the 1980's." In *Education and Rural Economic*

Development: Strategies for the 1990's, 40- 92. AGES 9153, U.S. Department of Agriculture, Economic Research Service, September.

McIntire, Robert J. 1996. "Revisions in Household Survey Data Effective February 1996." *Employment and Earnings*, March: 8-14.

Malecki, Edward J. 1991. *Technology and Economic Development: The Dynamics of Local, Regional, and National Change*. New York: Longman Scientific and Technical and John Wiley and Sons.

Mishel, Lawrence, Jared Bernstein, and John Schmitt. 1997. *The State of Working America, 1996–97*. Washington, DC: Economic Policy Institute.

Murphy, Kevin, and Finis Welch. 1989. "Wage Premiums for College Graduates: Recent Growth and Possible Explanations." *Educational Researcher* (May), pp. 17–26.

Topel, Robert H. 1997. "Factor Proportions and Relative Wages: The Supply-Side Determinants of Wage Inequality." *Journal of Economic Perspectives* 11, no. 2 (Spring):55–74.

U.S. Department of Commerce, Bureau of the Census. 1979. *Current Population Survey, March 1979* (machine readable data file). Conducted for the Bureau of Labor Statistics.

_____. 1990 *Current Population Survey, March 1990* (machine readable data file). Conducted for the Bureau of Labor Statistics.

_____. 1996. *Current Population Survey, March 1996* (machine readable data file). Conducted for the Bureau of Labor Statistics.

_____. 1993. *Census of Population and Housing, 1990. Public Use Microdata Sample B*. Bureau of the Census.

ABOUT THE AUTHORS

Dale Ballou is associate professor of economics at the University of Massachusetts. He received a Ph.D. in economics from Yale University in 1989. Ballou's research has focused on economic analyses of the determinants of teacher quality and school effectiveness. His work on teachers' pay, teacher effort, and education policy has appeared in such publications as the *Journal of Human Resources, Industrial and Labor Relations Review,* and the *Quarterly Journal of Economics. Teacher Pay and Teacher Quality,* a book coauthored with Michael Podgursky, was published by the W.E. Upjohn Institute in 1997.

Linda Ghelfi is a senior economist in the Food Assistance, Poverty, and Well-Being Branch, Economic Research Service. She holds a master's degree in public affairs, a combination of economic and political science, from the George Washington University. During her tenure at ERS, Ghelfi has researched rural income, poverty, and employment issues and served as executive editor of *Rural Development Perspectives* and *Rural Conditions and Trends,* and currently is investigating the role of food assistance in the quality of child care.

Robert Gibbs leads the rural labor group in the Food Assistance, Poverty, and Well Being Branch at the Economic Research Service in Washington, where he has worked as a regional economist since 1991. Both his dissertation, completed at the University of Pennsylvania, and his subsequent research have focused on youth migration and human capital formation. Gibbs' work has appeared in the *Journal of Regional Science, Review of Regional Studies,* and *Rural Development Perspectives.*

Elizabeth Greenberg is a research analyst at the American Institutes for Research in Washington, D.C. She holds a master's degree in political science from the University of California at Berkeley. During her 5 years at the Economic Research Service, she researched a range of issues concerning rural education policy.

David McGranahan leads the Rural Economy Team in the Food and Rural Economy Division, Economic Research Service. He also heads the ERS Rural Manufacturing Survey. Since completing a Ph.D. in sociology from the

University of Wisconsin, he has conducted research on a wide array of rural development issues, particularly job growth, industrial change, and human capital development. his work has appeared, among other places, in the *American Sociological Review*, the *Regional Science Review, Growth and Change*, and *Rural Sociology*.

Kathleen Paasch is a former member of the ERS rural labor group and currently completing her training in veterinary medicine at Washington State University in Pullman. She has published research on parent-child relationships, marriage, and family-influenced education choices in *Demography*, the *Journal of Family Issues,* and *Sociological Forum*. Paasch received a Ph.D. in sociology from the University of Maryland in 1992.

Michael Podgursky is chair of the Department of Economics, University of Missouri at Columbia. He has contributed numerous articles on education policy, teaching standards and remuneration, job training, and worker displacement to the *Journal of Labor Economics*, the *Journal of Human Resources*, and the *Monthly Labor Review*. *Teacher Pay and Teacher Quality*, a book coauthored with Dale Ballou, was published by the W.E. Upjohn Institute in 1997. Podgursky received a Ph.D. in economics from the University of Wisconsin.

Paul Swaim, a former leader of the rural labor group at ERS, is currently principal administrator in the Directorate for Education, Employment, Labour, and Social Affairs, at the Organization for Economic Cooperation and Development in Paris. A Ph.D. graduate in economics from the Massachusetts Institute of Technology, Swaim has written extensively on displaced workers, earnings mobility, rural employment, and job training. His research has appeared in such publications as the *Journal of Human Resources,* the *Journal of Labor Economics*, and the *Review of Economics and Statistics*.

Ruy Teixeira is director of the Politics and Public Opinion Program at the Economic Policy Institute in Washington, D.C. He is also a former visiting fellow at the Brookings Institution. Since receiving his doctorate from the University of Wisconsin, he has become a nationally-recognized authority on American voting patterns, and has also published a sizable body of research on worker education, training, and skills. His writings have appeared in a variety of monographs, journals, magazines, and newspapers, including the *American Journal of Education*, the *American Journal of Sociology*, the *New York Times*, the *American Enterprise*, and the *Brookings Review*.

ACKNOWLEDGMENTS

We would like to thank the Cooperative State Research Service (now CSREES), United States Department of Agriculture, for funding our original project on rural education and training under the National Research Initiative Competitive Grants Program (grant # 92-37401-8281).

A special debt of gratitude is owed to the Economic Research Service, also in USDA, for its continuing support during all phases of the preparation of this manuscript. While USDA enabled this research, the opinions expressed in this book are those of the authors alone.

Although we have received advice and assistance from many persons, we would be especially remiss if we did not mention the enormous efforts of Linda Ghelfi, one of the book's contributors, whose thorough review and revision of an earlier version of the manuscript made the editors' work so much easier later on. In the final stages of preparation, the book benefited greatly from a close reading by Kathleen Kassel of ERS, who also prepared the camera copy. Linda and Kathleen held us to high standards of cogency and readability. All remaining lapses in those standards are entirely the responsibility of the editors.

INDEX

Absenteeism in schools, 143, 161
Abuse, physical and verbal, 12-14
Achievement. *See* Educational achievement
Advanced education, 6-7
Age as literacy factor, 86-87, 93
Agricultural industry, 133-135. *See also*
    Production industries
Alcohol abuse. *See* Substance abuse
Apprenticeship programs, 54, 58
Attendance. *See* College attendance
Attitudes, 125, 129

Beale codes, 24
    categorization of urbanization, 95
    interpretation of, 37
    SASS data and, 4-5
Bilingual courses, 7
Boston Compact, 54
Brain drain. *See* Migration; Workforce

Careers. *See also* Jobs
    college characteristics and, 73, 78
    occupational expectations of students, 54-56
Census use in trend analysis, 157-163
Collective bargaining. *See* Unionization of
    teachers
College attendance
    family income and, 67, 69-70
    graduation and, 65, 78
    probability, 71-72
College graduation. *See also* Graduation rates
    earning trends and, 147-150, 153
    effect of geographical distances, 73
    job requirements upon, 138-139, 141
    population levels, 143-146
College loans and grants, 67
Community, 68, 70, 72
Comparisons of rural vs. urban schools
    collective bargaining, 11
    educational achievement, 24-28
    educational attainment, 63-66
    high school dropout rates, 42-44, 47, 50-51
    occupational expectations of students, 54-56

school assessments, 15
school problems, 14
student/teacher ratio, 8
teacher characteristics, 11
teacher influence, 16
teacher salaries, 9
Consolidation of rural schools, 4-6
Consumer services industries
    change in education level of, 138-140
    earnings trends in, 147, 150-151
    educational requirements in, 142-143
    effect of educational requirements on, 155-156
    explanation of categories in, 165
    rural/urban roles in, 133-136
Current Population Survey (CPS), 98, 101-102, 157-163
Curriculum
    course offerings, 31-32
    educational achievement by region, 26-27
    school size and, 6-7
    teacher influence and, 16

Data sources. *See* Schools and Staffing
    Survey; Surveys
Demographics
    dropout rates and, 58
    effect of college location on community, 68, 70, 72
    in determining rural migration, 63
    use in analysis of Beale codes, 37
    workforce literacy and, 88, 90-91
Document literacy
    literacy testing and, 83, 86-88, 92
Dropout rates
    by age and risk factors, 47
    effect of parental behavior and, 49-52
    income and, 49-52, 56
    migration and, 73
    NELS dropout survey, 45-48, 57
    recent trends, 42-43
Dropouts
    analysis of causes, 48-52, 57
    peripheral effects of, 41
Drug abuse. *See* Substance abuse